AF256653

CONTENTS

INTRODUCTION

My story has started a long time before I decided to be slim. Ever since childhood, I was overweight. During the teen time, my situation wasn't so deplorable. I am grateful to my family because they always accepted me as I am. But it wasn't enough for me because all around hated me. At the age of 15, I understood that I am unshapely girl. I was in graduation class, my weight has already exceeded 270 lbs. I felt like I am a giant cow who couldn't fit into any sexy dress for a prom party. My parents have never been worried about weight, they just repeated all the time "you are an angel, you are beautiful". I knew that it wasn't true, in the mirror I saw plum girl. After graduating from school, I became very depressed. All my troubles I jammed with tones of chocolate and Coke.

One sunny day I firmly decided for myself - enough for me! I don't want to live like that anymore. I will be changed. I had made the "wish map", where I was slim and smiling, and started to do sports and eat fewer sweets and sparkling drinks. I couldn't say that it wasn't successful but I didn't get the desired result. I wanted everything at once, so I even practiced fasting. I could drink water and vegetable smoothies for 2-3 days. But it all ended with me breaking down and gaining even more weight. At that time, I already started having health problems. I could not walk for a long time, I was haunted by headaches, pain in my stomach, as well as bad breath.

I decided to go to the doctor and do a comprehensive analysis of the whole body. When my doctor looked at my tests, hc adviscd going to a nutritionist. This time I discovered a ketogenic diet. The doctor didn't prescribe something special. It was a certain diet and simple physical exercises every day. But I have to eat a lot of proteins, and almost no vegetables (I hated them at that time). I couldn't believe that everything is so easy! But I didn't lose faith and clearly followed the doctor's instructions. After a week of keto life, I did not see significant results, but after 2 weeks the arrows of the scales showed -8 lbs. During the year of keto lifestyle, my weight dropped by 83 lbs and my health became better. I cried with happiness! Finally, I did it! This is just a miracle! Now I am a wife, mom, and just happy woman!

I wrote this book to help people like me. To those who still think that they are hopeless! I am sure that this diet will change your way of thinking and make a big difference in your life. I am the greatest example that nothing is impossible. You should know that losing weight is not only restrictions and starving. The real-life on keto diet exists and this book proves it! Our mind and our body are omnipotent! They know well what we need! Each of us should be dropkicked to take the path of a happy life! I strongly believe that this book will be a guide and silver lining in a better version of you!

WHAT TO EAT AND AVOID ON THE KETO DIET

Meat and poultry

Actually, it is the primary type of food for the Keto diet. It contains 0% of carbs and is rich in potassium, selenium, zinc, and B vitamins. Grass-fed meat and poultry are the most beneficial. It caused by high omega 3 fats and antioxidants content. Bear in mind that Keto diet is a high-fat diet and high consumption of proteins can cause to harder getting of ketosis.

What to eat	Enjoy occasionally	What to avoid
<ul><li>chicken</li><li>duck</li><li>goose</li><li>ground beef</li><li>lamb</li><li>ostrich</li><li>partridge</li><li>pheasant</li><li>pork</li><li>quail</li><li>turkey</li><li>venison</li></ul>	<ul><li>bacon</li><li>ham</li><li>low-fat meat, such as skinless chicken breast</li><li>sausage</li></ul>	<ul><li>breaded meats</li><li>processed meats</li></ul>

Dairy

High-fat dairy products are awesome for the keto diet. They are calcium-rich full-fat dairy product is nutritious and can make you full longer. Milk lovers should restrict or even cross out this product from the daily meal plan. It is allowed only 1 tablespoon of milk in your drink per day but doesn't abuse it daily.

What to eat	What to avoid
butter	fat-free yogurt
cheese (soft and hard)	low-fat cheese
full-fat yogurt	milk
heavy cream	skim milk
sour cream	skim mozzarella
	sweetened yogurt

Eggs

This is the most wholesome food in the world. Use them everywhere you want! Containing less than one gram of carbohydrates, eggs are a wonderful food for the keto lifestyle. Eating eggs reducing the risk of heart disease and save your eyes health.

Note: free-range eggs are healthier options for the keto diet.

What to avoid	
chicken eggs	ostrich eggs
duck eggs	quail eggs
goose eggs	

Fish and Seafood

Fatty fish as salmon is beneficial for the keto diet. Small fish like sardines, herring, etc. are less in toxins. The best option for a keto diet is wild-caught seafood; it has a higher number of omega 3 fats. Scientifically proved that frequent eating of fish improves mental health.

What to eat		What to avoid
catfish	prawns	breaded fish
clams	salmon	
cod	sardines	
crab	scallops	
halibut	shrimp	
herring	snapper	
lobster	swordfish	
mackerel	tilapia	
Mahi Mahi	trout	
mussels	tuna	
oysters		

Nuts and Seeds

These products are heart-healthy and fiber-rich. Nevertheless, eat nuts and seeds as a snack is a bad idea. As usual, the amount of eaten food can be much more than allowed. Nuts like cashews are very insidious and contain a lot of carbohydrates. Replace them with macadamia or pecan.

What to eat		What to avoid
almonds	peanuts	cashews
chia seeds	pecans	pistachio
flaxseeds	pumpkin seeds	chocolate-covered nuts
hazelnuts	walnuts	nut butter (sweetened)
nut butter (unsweetened)	macadamia nuts	

Oils and fats

It is the main component of the keto-friendly sauces and dressings.

Olive oil and coconut oil are highly recommending for everyone who decided to follow the keto diet. They are almost perfect it their fatty acid composition. Avoid artificial trans fats which are poison for our body. This type of fats, as usual, used in French fries, margarine, and crackers.

What to eat	What to avoid
• avocado oil	• grapeseed oil
• coconut oil	• canola oil
• hazelnut oil	• cottonseed oil
• olive oil	• hydrogenated oils
• pumpkin seed oil	• margarine
• sesame oil	• peanut oil
• walnut oil	• soybean oil
	• safflower oil
	• processed vegetable oils

Vegetables

Keto diet cannot work without vegetables, but their usage should be in moderation. Starchy vegetables such as potatoes, sweet potatoes, etc. are deadly for our body and will not bring anything more than overweight. At the same time, vegetables that are low in carbs, are rich in antioxidants and can protect the body from free radicals that damage our cells.

What to eat		What to avoid
• asparagus	• mushrooms	• carrots
• avocado	• olives	• corn
• broccoli	• onions	• beets
• cabbage	• tomatoes	• butternut squash
• cauliflower	• peppers	• parsnips
• celery	• spinach	• potatoes (both sweet and regular)
• cucumber	• zucchini	
• eggplant	• other nonstarchy vegetables	• pumpkin
• leafy greens		• turnips
• lettuce		• yams
		• yuca
		• other starchy vegetables

Fruits

This type of food is high in carbs that's why they should be limited while keto diet. Besides this, almost all fruits are high in glucose and can enhance blood sugar.

Enjoy occasionally	What to avoid	
• lemons	• apples	• peaches
• pomegranates	• bananas	• pears
• limes	• grapefruits	• pineapple
	• limes	• plums
	• mango	• dried fruits
	• oranges	

Berries

If you are looking for how to substitute fruits, this is your godsend. Berries contain up to 12 grams of net carbs per 3.5 ounces serving. They are high in fiber and can maintain the health of your body and fight with diseases. Note consumption of a huge amount of berries can be harmful.

Enjoy occasionally	What to avoid
• blackberries	• cherries
• blueberries	• grapes
• raspberries	• melon
• strawberries	• watermelon

Beans and legumes

There are no ingredients in this food group that would be healthy for a keto diet. Beans and legumes contain fewer carbs in comparison with root vegetables such as potatoes; nevertheless, this type of carbohydrates fastly adds up.

What to avoid	
• black beans	• navy beans
• chickpeas	• peas
• kidney beans	• pinto beans
• lentils	• soybeans

Condiments

Condiments can make any type of meal awesome. Even a piece of meat will turn into the masterpiece with them. There are only a few products which are better to avoid; nevertheless, nowadays, you can find keto-friendly substitutors in a supermarket.

One more hot tip: putting hot pepper in your meal will reduce the amount of salt you need and make the taste of the dish more saturated.

What to eat	What to avoid
• herbs and spices	• BBQ sauce
• lemon juice	• hot sauces
• mayonnaise with no added sugar	• ketchup
• salad dressings with no added sugar	• maple syrup
• salt and pepper	• salad dressings with added sugar
• vinegar	• sweet dipping sauces
	• tomato sauce

Grain products

Actually, it is needless to say that all grains are forbidden and can't be eaten if you want to achieve ketosis. Grains contain complex carbohydrates that have a feature to be absorbed slower than simple carbohydrates. For better understanding, if the food has keto-friendly carbs, look at the number of starch and sugar. Their number should be minimum.

What to avoid	
• baked goods	• muesli
• bread	• oats
• cereal	• pasta
• corn	• pizza
• crackers	• popcorn
• flour	• rice
• granola	• wheat

Beverages

A variety of keto drinks may shock you. Probably you know that the best beverage for a keto diet is water. Nevertheless, in order to brighten up a little gray everyday life of keto lovers, the consumption of alcoholic beverages is allowed in moderation. For instance, pure forms of alcohol, such as gin, vodka, or tequila can be drunk once per week. They contain zero amounts of carbs. Avoid all sweetened beverages; they are a priori high carbohydrate.

What to eat	Enjoy occasionally	What to avoid
• almond milk	• dry wine	• alcoholic drinks (sweetened)
• bone broth	• hard liquor	• beer
• coffee (unsweetened)	• vodka	• cider
• flax milk	• other low carb alcoholic drinks	• coffee (sweetened)
• tea (unsweetened)		• fruit juice
• water (still and sparkling)		• soda
		• sports drinks
		• smoothies
		• tea (sweetened)
		• wines (sweet)

Sweets

Cakes and cookies cannot help in losing weight in any diet. As for keto, here everything is strict with this. You should try to avoid sugar and sweeteners in any form. Moreover, sweets negatively affect blood sugar and insulin levels.

Enjoy occasionally	What to avoid	
• erythritol	• artificial sweeteners	• ice cream
• stevia	• buns	• pastries
• sucralose	• candy	• pies
	• cakes	• pudding
	• chocolate	• sugar
	• cookies	• tarts
	• custard	

Others

Fast food and processed food contain a huge amount of stabilizers and harmful carbohydrates. The main rule of the Keto diet is avoiding sugar. 99,9% of such food contains harmful sugars. The existence of which in the body negates the achievement of ketosis.

What to avoid

• fast food
• processed foods

TOP 10 INSTANT POT TIPS

1. Flavored liquids enhance your meal.

Broths, juices, dairies, and stocks can enhance the taste of your meal. This kind of liquids has the property not only to convey its taste but also the taste of spices that were used while cooking. Don't be afraid of experiments! The mixture of chicken beef broth and sautéed garlic instead of ordinary water will turn the lean rice on a flavored meal.

2. Cook by small pieces instead of the whole product.

You can reduce the cooking time almost two times by chopping the ingredients into small pieces. Doing this, the pressure and steam will reach the ingredients evenly and will cook them faster.

3. Make the sauces and gravies after cooking.

Thickening liquids is a good way to get delicious gravies; they can improve the taste of your dish. The best liquid thickeners are starch and flour. Adding them in the last minutes of cooking will make the texture of the meal more saturated and uniform. Also, this method helps not to overcook the ingredients, do not deprive them of vitamins and as a result, make the food healthier.

4. A steaming rack is a good option for any meal.

Almost all Instant pot models come with steamer rack that is essential not only for cooking vegetables. This tool can be appropriate at any time when you want to cook the ingredients with less amount of liquids. Such food as pies, fish, or meat will have a completely different taste if you use steamer rack while cooking.

5. Use improvised things.

Nowadays, the market suggests a huge variety of accessories for instant pot. Some of them have important meaning but some can be substitute by simple things. For instance, foil can be a wonderful replacement for instant pot trays and molds. It can take any form and has non-stick features. Use it for cooking muffins, pies, and even meatloaves.

6. Cooking with pressure can take more time.

As a rule, it takes approximately 10-15 minutes to reach the needed pressure in the inner pot. Very rarely the recipes include this time in the total cooking time; that's to accurately determine the cooking time and notify your family when it is time to eat, add extra minutes to the cooking time specified in the recipe.

7. **Cook two or more meals per one time.**

The instant pot comes with only one inner pot, which is not always convenient when cooking several dishes. Therefore, nimble housewives found an excellent life hack on how to save time not only on cooking but also on washing dishes. To do this, simply purchase a few more inner pots and cook meals more quickly.

8. **Get rid of odors.**

Using the sealing rings will help you to avoid the odors. As usual, the smell of spices after cooking meat, fish, or vegetable meals are very strong. That's why it is highly recommended to buy extra sealing rings for all the most popular types of meal you cook; so each dish can retain its unique taste and flavor.

9. **Easy cleaning.**

Use a dishwasher to wash all removable parts of the instant pot. Detergent and a strong flow of water in the dishwasher will make your instant pot clean and at the same time save your time. For non-removable instant pot parts, use vinegar and lemon juice. They can make your kitchen appliance sparkle like new.

10. **Clean nooks, so instant pot is always like new.**

Sometimes the nooks of instant pot become clogged with sauces, steam after using pressure cooking mode or food leftovers that were accidentally spilled. Clean the nooks with the help of the brush and paper after each usage of the instant pot to preserve its original appearance for many years.

TOP 10 KETO DIET TIPS

1.   Combine together Keto and Intermittent fasting.

Intermittent fasting (IF) is the right way to get ketosis. It gives your body additional benefits.
Scientists showed that connection keto diet and intermittent fasting can up the results which can give only strict following of the keto diet.

IF means not eating and drinking during a determined amount of time. It is recommended to separate your day into a building phase (BP) and cleansing phase(CP); where the building phase is the time between the first and last time of eating (first-last); and cleansing is the opposite time (last-first). Start from 14-hours CP and 11-hours BP. Continue like this till your body adapts to the new daily plan. It can take 2-3 days. The first days will be the hardest but then you will feel relief and you can safely proceed to the next stage where BP turns into 5 hours and CP - into 19 hours.

According to research, women get the highest benefits of IF. It is possible to get rid of adrenal fatigue, hypothyroid, and hormonal imbalance.

2.   Staying hydrated is essential.

Our body is 60% water. Water ensures the normal digestion of food and the absorption of nutrients from the intestines. If there is not enough water in the body, there will be discomfort in the abdomen and constipation. Drinking water is important even if you are not on keto.

The kidneys filter 5,000 ounces of blood per day so that the result is 50 ounces of urine. For the normal elimination of toxins and waste substances, you need to drink at least 50 ounces of water per day, but preferably more.

Many people face the problem of unwillingness to drink water. The best way to prevent dehydration and all its unpleasant consequences is to put a bottle or cup of water on the table and take a sip every time you look at the water. If you realize that you are thirsty, then eliminate thirst in time.

Regular drinking of the right amount of water for 1 week will become a habit and you will not be able to live differently.

3.   Salt isn't harmful.

Salt plays an important role in complex metabolic processes. It is part of the blood, lymph, saliva, tears, gastric juice, bile - that is, all the fluids of our body. Any fluctuations in the salt content in the blood plasma lead to serious metabolic disorders

When fewer carbohydrates enter the body, insulin levels drop. Less insulin circulating in the body leads to secrete excess water in the kidneys instead of holding it. It means that salt and other important minerals and electrolytes are washed out of the body.

Replenish salt is possible by eating bone broths, cucumbers, celeriac, salty keto nuts, and seeds.

The best salts for keto diet are 2 types of salt. Pink salt has a more saturated, saltier taste, and contains calcium, magnesium, and potassium. Sea salt is simply evaporated seawater. The crystals of sea salt are slightly larger than iodized salt, and it has a stronger aroma. It contains potassium, magnesium, sulfur, phosphorus, and zinc.

4. Sport is important.

It is proved that physical activity improves the health of the whole body in general and accelerates metabolism. When we do sport, the first thing is we get rid of carbohydrates, and only then we burn fats. On a keto diet, even minimal physical activity contributes to the rapid decomposition of fats. You simply don't have glucose (carbohydrates) and any load breaks down fats. The most effective workouts on an empty stomach. Sports during keto are very comfortable. You do not feel hungry and can play sports without breakdowns and overeating. Your stamina is significantly increased. If the protein is correctly calculated, you don't lose muscle mass with a calorie deficit.

The combination of three types of workouts gives the best result for health, weight dynamics, and even mood! These are workouts, aerobic, and stretching. Start with small loads every day and increase it as you can. Do not forget to take measurements of your body to monitor the result!

5. Reduce stress.

Sometimes, observing all the postulates of the keto lifestyle, ketosis does not occur or occurs very slowly. In 99 cases, it happens due to the level of stress in your life. Thus, the hormone cortisol rises, the sympathetic nervous system is stimulated.

Cortisol is produced in response to any stress, even the most minor. How does it happen?

Cortisol "eats" our muscles to turn them into glucose, it catabolizes bones, which is fraught with osteoporosis, causes increased appetite, and suppresses immunity. It also causes increased production of glucose and insulin, and exactly this stops ketosis.

During keto-adaptation (the first 3 weeks), increased cortisol is produced, because the usual energy, glucose, ceases to flow into the body, and it turns on the "self-preservation mode".

It is very important at first to minimize stress from the outside, then everything will normalize.

You should be able to switch from stimulation of the sympathetic nervous system to parasympathetic. Stimulation of the parasympathetic nervous system contributes to the restoration and accumulation of energy resources. This can be achieved by a simple 15 minutes' meditation. The time when you cannot be interrupted.

6.   Sleep above all!

Sleep and stress are two interconnected components. Lack of sleep leads to increased stress. Consequently, stress hormone levels and blood sugar levels rise and we gain weight very fast.

Doctors recommend an 8-9 hour sleep every day. The best time to fall asleep is before 11 pm. An hour before bedtime, try not to use any gadgets. It is better to spend this time in silence, meditation, listening to calm music or reading a paper book. Thus, we calm the nervous system and set it to sleep. If your stress level per day was high, try to spend more time sleeping. it is the sleep that contributes to our weight loss and getting rid of all diseases. There are some tips to improve your sleep comfort:

- Keep cool in the room. The optimum temperature should not exceed 65-70F.
- Use a black mask for sleeping and earplugs.
- Provide good room ventilation.

7.   Don't forget about vegetables.

It is obvious that the main resource of vitamins and minerals is vegetables. You can't cross out them totally from daily meals. Consuming them during the keto diet is very important, but should be in moderation. Starchy vegetables such as sweet potatoes and potatoes are not allowed. Nevertheless, at the same time, you can safely substitute them with broccoli, kale, spinach, white cabbage, Brussels sprouts to your diet. Such vegetables are not only low-carb, but also low-calorie and have a huge number of vitamins, antioxidants, and minerals. They will help you stay full for a long time and protect from eating an extra serving of nuts.

One of the tips of keto coaches is to pamper yourself with low-carb berries once a week. At the same time, it is very important to increase physical activity during this day. Cycling will be just right. All this will fill your body with useful antioxidants and will not add extra pounds.

8.   MCT oil is a treasure for a keto diet.

MCT oil is medium-chain triglyceride oil. It practically doesn't require splitting in the small intestine and is absorbed already in the duodenum, going directly to the liver. MCT oil is used by the body as an energy source, which leads to an increase in fat loss. On the other hand, MCT oil isn't deposited in body fat like fatty tissue in comparison with other fatty acids, and it has been shown that it improves thermogenesis, that is, the process during which the body creates heat using excess energy.

MCT oils are good for cooking, especially for baking, frying or grilling. This is due to their high point of "smoke", which means that they are very difficult to oxidize from heat and can withstand high temperatures without losing their original chemical structure at room temperature (losing their useful properties). You can also add MTC oil in keto shakes, coffee, tea, and other keto drinks.

9. Do a kitchen audit

The key to getting ketosis is proper low-carb nutrition. Nevertheless, our brain, knowing that somewhere in the fridge or freezer are a bar of chocolate or a package of vanilla ice cream. So it unconsciously creates situations in which we are obliged to eat them. That's why there are no doubts that one of the best tips is to clean your kitchen and all the shelves from the "seducers". Firstly, write a list of food that is not allowed during the diet, and then one by one throw away everything that is on your list. It may seem too radical right away. But just know that all this will help you completely switch to keto life faster and less stressfully for your body. Also, you can make a list of all you have in the fridge and stick this sheet of paper on the fridge. Doing this you will not eat extra snacks during the day.

10. Keep food near you.

Our life is full of events and sometimes we just don't have time to cook. We have a choice to buy high carbohydrate food in the shop or cook the right food by ourselves. All of this needs extra time. That's why you should always have a "healthy snack" with you. No matter what it is. It can be fat bombs, seeds, or nuts. If you have more time, make the keto salads, or find the keto fruits such as avocado and cook the spreads and dips. But bear in mind, you shouldn't cook much in advance. Their expired date is very short. Follow the rule to purchasing all ingredients for snacks in advance, so that they are always in your fridge. This way you can less likely break your diet and get rid of unnecessary overeating. If you don't know what to cook, use the recipe generator which can help you with the meal for your certain list of food.

BREAKFAST

Chicken Strips

Prep time: 10 minutes | **Cook time:** 15 minutes | **Yield:** 5 servings

Ingredients

1-pound chicken fillet

½ teaspoon ground turmeric

½ teaspoon salt

½ teaspoon ground black pepper

2 tablespoons heavy cream

1 cup of coconut milk

1 teaspoon olive oil

Method

1.	Cut the chicken fillet into the strips and sprinkle with ground turmeric, salt, ground black pepper, and heavy cream.

2.	Preheat the olive oil on saute mode for 3 minutes,

3.	Then place the chicken strips in hot oil in one layer. Cook them for 1 minute from each side and add coconut cream.

4.	Close and seal the lid.

5.	Cook the chicken strips on Manual (high pressure) for 10 minutes. Make a quick pressure release.

Nutritional info per serve: calories 313, fat 21.3, fiber 1.2, carbs 3.1, protein 27.5

Nut Yogurt

Prep time: 10 minutes | **Cook time:** 6 minutes | **Yield:** 3 servings

Ingredients

1 cup of coconut yogurt

½ oz pistachio nuts, chopped

½ oz hazelnuts, chopped

½ oz macadamia nuts, chopped

1 teaspoon Erythritol

½ teaspoon coconut oil

Method

1.	Preheat the coconut oil on saute mode for 1 minute.

2.	When the oil is hot, add pistachio nuts, hazelnuts, and macadamia nuts. Cook them on saute mode for 5 minutes. Stir the nuts constantly.

3.	Then cool the buts well and mix them up with Erythritol and coconut yogurt.

4.	Put the cooked meal in the serving jars.

Nutritional info per serve: calories 132, fat 10.7, fiber 1.3, carbs 8.9, protein 3.3

Chili Roasted Eggs

Prep time: 5 minutes | **Cook time:** 7 minutes | **Yield:** 3 servings

Ingredients

1 teaspoon coconut oil

3 eggs

½ teaspoon chili flakes

Method

1.	Heat up coconut oil in the instant pot on Saute mode.

2.	When the coconut oil is hot, crack the eggs in the instant pot bowl and sprinkle with chili flakes.

3.	Cook the eggs on saute mode for 5 minutes.

Nutritional info per serve: calories 76, fat 5.9, fiber 0, carbs 0.4, protein 5.5

Feta Stuffed Chicken

Prep time: 15 minutes | **Cook time:** 17 minutes | **Yield:** 5 servings

Ingredients

1-pound chicken breast, skinless, boneless

1 tablespoon Italian seasonings

1 teaspoon olive oil

3 oz Feta cheese, crumbled

1 cup water, for cooking

Method

1.   Beat the chicken breast gently with the help of the kitchen hammer.

2.   Then make a cut in the breast (to get the pocket).

3.   Rub the chicken with Italian seasonings and olive oil.

4.   Then fill the "chicken pocket" with crumbled Feta.

5.   After this, wrap the chicken breast in the foil.

6.   Pour water and insert the steamer rack in the instant pot.

7.   Place the chicken on the rack; close and seal the lid

8.   Cook the meal on manual mode (high pressure) for 17 minutes; allow the natural pressure release for 5 minutes.

Nutritional info per serve: calories 165, fat 7.7, fiber 0, carbs 1, protein 21.7

Pancetta Eggs

Prep time: 10 minutes | **Cook time:** 5 minutes | **Yield:** 4 servings

Ingredients

2 oz Pancetta, fried

4 eggs

1 teaspoon chives, chopped

½ teaspoon salt

Cooking spray

1 cup water, for cooking

Method

1.   Spray the egg molds with cooking spray.

2.   Crack the eggs in the egg molds and sprinkle with salt, chives, and Pancetta. Stir every egg mixture gently.

3.   Then pour water and insert the steamer rack in the instant pot.

4.   Put the egg molds in the instant pot. Close and seal the lid.

5.   Cook the meal on manual mode (high pressure) for 5 minutes. Make a quick pressure release.

Nutritional info per serve: calories 140, fat 10.3, fiber 0, carbs 0.6, protein 10.8

Cupcake Mugs

Prep time: 20 minutes | **Cook time:** 17 minutes | **Yield:** 6 servings

Ingredients

4 eggs, beaten

½ teaspoon ground cinnamon

½ teaspoon vanilla extract

1 cup almond flour

1 teaspoon baking powder

1/3 cup coconut cream

2 tablespoon Erythritol

1 teaspoon butter, melted

1 cup water, for cooking

Method

1. Mix up together all ingredients and pour the mixture in the glass jars.

2. Then pour water and insert the steamer rack in the instant pot.

3. Cover every glass jar with foil and secure the edges.

4. Then place the jars on the rack. Close and seal the lid.

5. Cook the cupcake mugs on Manual (high pressure) for 17 minutes.

6. Then make a quick pressure release and let the cooked meal cool for 10 minutes before serving.

Nutritional info per serve: calories 192, fat 15.6, fiber 2.4, carbs 10.6, protein 8

Cauliflower Quiche

Prep time: 10 minutes | **Cook time:** 10 minutes | **Yield:** 2 servings

Ingredients

1 cup cauliflower, chopped

¼ cup Cheddar cheese, shredded

5 eggs, beaten

1 teaspoon butter

1 teaspoon dried oregano

1 cup of water

Method

1. Grease the instant pot baking pan with butter from inside.

2. Pour water in the instant pot.

3. Sprinkle the cauliflower with dried oregano and put it in the prepared baking pan. Flatten the vegetables gently.

4. After this, add eggs and stir the vegetables.

5. Top the quiche with shredded cheese and transfer it in the instant pot. Close and seal the lid.

6. Cook the quiche on manual mode (high pressure) for 10 minutes. Make a quick pressure release.

Nutritional info per serve: calories 246, fat 17.7, fiber 1.6, carbs 4.2, protein 18.5

Chicken Frittata

Prep time: 10 minutes | **Cook time:** 6 minutes | **Yield:** 2 servings

Ingredients

3 eggs, beaten

4 oz chicken fillet, boiled

1 teaspoon coconut oil

¼ teaspoon cayenne pepper

1 cup water, for cooking

Method

1. Pour water in the instant pot.

2. Then shred the boiled chicken fillet and mix it up with eggs, coconut oil, and cayenne pepper.

3. Pour the mixture in the instant pot baking mold and transfer it in the instant pot.

4. Close and seal the lid and cook the frittata on manual mode (high pressure) for 6 minutes.

5. When the time of cooking is finished, make a quick pressure release and cut the frittata into servings.

Nutritional info per serve: calories 222, fat 13.1, fiber 0.1, carbs 0.6, protein 24.7

Vegetable Frittata

Prep time: 10 minutes | **Cook time:** 10 minutes | **Yield:** 4 servings

Ingredients

4 eggs, beaten

2 oz Pecorino cheese, grated

3 oz okra, chopped

2 oz radish, chopped

1 tablespoon cream cheese

1 teaspoon sesame oil

Method

1.	Heat up sesame oil in the instant pot on saute mode.

2.	Add chopped okra and radish and saute the vegetables for 4 minutes.

3.	Then stir them well and add cream cheese and beaten eggs.

4.	Stir the mixture well and top with cheese.

5.	Close the lid and cook the frittata on saute mode for 6 minutes more.

Nutritional info per serve: calories 163, fat 12.1, fiber 0.9, carbs 2.5, protein 11.9

Egg&Cheese

Prep time: 10 minutes | **Cook time:** 6 minutes | **Yield:** 1 serving

Ingredients

2 eggs, beaten

1 oz Parmesan, grated

1 oz Swiss cheese, grated

¼ cup heavy cream

½ teaspoon dried cilantro

½ teaspoon almond butter

Method

1.	Toss the almond butter in the instant pot and melt it on saute mode.

2.	Then add eggs and cream cheese. Sprinkle the ingredients with dried cilantro and cook on saute mode for 4 minutes.

3.	When the egg mixture is solid, stir it gently to get the small egg pieces.

4.	After this, add grated cheese and close the lid. Cook the meal for 2 minutes more.

Nutritional info per serve: calories 192, fat 15.6, fiber 2.4, carbs 10.6, protein 8

Ham Muffins

Prep time: 10 minutes | **Cook time:** 6 minutes | **Yield:** 2 servings

Ingredients

2 eggs, beaten

4 oz ham, chopped

½ teaspoon avocado oil

1 cup water, for cooking

Method

1.	Pour water in the instant pot.

2.	Then brush the muffin molds with avocado oil from inside.

3.	In the mixing bowl, mix up ham and beaten eggs.

4.	After this, pour the mixture into the muffin molds.

5.	Place the muffins in the instant pot. Close and seal the lid.

6.	Cook the meal on manual mode (high pressure) for 6 minutes. Then make a quick pressure release and remove the muffins.

Nutritional info per serve: calories 192, fat 15.6, fiber 2.4, carbs 10.6, protein 8

Mushroom Toast

Prep time: 10 minutes | **Cook time:** 12 minutes | **Yield:** 3 servings

Ingredients

1 cup mushrooms, grinded

2 eggs, beaten

2 tablespoons coconut flour

1 tablespoon chives, chopped

1 tablespoon butter

Method

1.   In the mixing bowl, mix up grinded mushrooms, eggs, coconut flour, and chives.

2.   Stir the mixture with the help of the spoon until it is homogenous.

3.   Then melt butter in the instant pot on saute mode.

4.   With the help of the spoon make the medium size toasts from the mushroom mixture and place them in the hot butter.

5.   Saute the toasts for 5 minutes from each side.

Nutritional info per serve: calories 121, fat 8.2 fiber 3.6, carbs 6.4, protein 5.8

Spanakopita

Prep time: 20 minutes | **Cook time:** 15 minutes | **Yield:** 4 servings

Ingredients

½ cup coconut flour

3 eggs, beaten

2 tablespoons goat milk butter

1 cup spinach, chopped

1 oz scallions, chopped

3 tablespoons cream cheese

4 egg whites, whisked

1 cup water, for cooking

Method

1.   Make the dough: in the mixing bowl mix up coconut flour, eggs, and goat milk butter. Knead the dough.

2.   Then place the dough in the round mold and flatten in the shape of the pie crust.

3.   Pour water in the instant pot and insert the steamer rack.

4.   Put the mold with the pie crust on the rack. Close and seal the lid. Cook the pie crust for 10 minutes on manual mode (high pressure) + quick pressure release.

5.   After this, mix up spinach, scallions, cream cheese, and eggs,

6.   Pour the mixture over the cooked pie crust.

7.   Cook the spanakopita for 5 minutes more on manual mode (high pressure). Then allow the natural pressure release for 5 minutes.

Nutritional info per serve: calories 157, fat 12.3, fiber 1, carbs 2.5, protein 8.9

3-Cheese Quiche Cups

Prep time: 10 minutes | **Cook time:** 6 minutes | **Yield:** 6 servings

Ingredients

6 eggs, beaten

2 tablespoon cream cheese

1 teaspoon Italian seasonings

¼ cup Cheddar cheese, shredded

3 oz Monterey Jack cheese, shredded

2 oz Mozzarella, shredded

1 cup water, for cooking

Method

1.   Pour water in the instant pot.

2.   In the mixing bowl, mix up eggs cream cheese, Italian seasonings, and all types of cheese.

3.   Pour the mixture in the baking cups (molds) and place them in the instant pot.

4.   Close and seal the lid.

5.   Cook the quiche cups for 6 minutes on manual mode (high pressure).

6.   Make a quick pressure release.

Nutritional info per serve: calories 175, fat 13.3, fiber 1, carbs 1, protein 13.1

Sausage Puffs

Prep time: 15 minutes | **Cook time:** 10 minutes | **Yield:** 6 servings

Ingredients

9 oz ground sausages, fried

1 egg, beaten

¼ cup coconut flour

¼ teaspoon baking powder

3 oz Provolone cheese, grated

1 tablespoon cream cheese

1 cup water, for cooking

Method

1.   In the mixing bowl, mix up ground sausages, egg, coconut flour, baking powder, grated Parmesan, and cream cheese.

2.   Make the small puff from the ground sausages and put in the non-stick baking pan.

3.   Pour water and insert the pan with sausage puffs in the instant pot.

4.   Close and seal the lid.

5.   Cook the meal on manual (high pressure) for 10 minutes. Make a quick pressure release.

Nutritional info per serve: calories 230, fat 17.8, fiber 1.7, carbs 3.2, protein 13.6

Cheddar Muffins

Prep time: 10 minutes | **Cook time:** 12 minutes | **Yield:** 3 servings

Ingredients

2 oz Cheddar cheese, shredded

2 tablespoons almond flour

2 tablespoon butter, softened

1 tablespoon heavy cream

¼ teaspoon baking powder

½ teaspoon lemon juice

1 cup water, for cooking

Method

1.   Pour water in the instant pot.

2.   Then mix up together all remaining ingredients and stir until homogenous.

3.   Put the muffin batter in the muffin molds and insert them in the instant pot.

4.   Close and seal the lid.

5.   Cook the Cheddar muffins for 12 minutes on high pressure (manual mode).

6.   When the time is finished, make a quick pressure release.

Nutritional info per serve: calories 269, fat 25.1, fiber 2, carbs 4.6, protein 8.9

Spicy Eggs

Prep time: 5 minutes | **Cook time:** 3 minutes |
Yield: 2 servings

Ingredients

4 eggs

¾ teaspoon chili powder

¼ teaspoon jalapeno pepper

1 teaspoon cream cheese

Method

1.   Pour 1 cup of water in the instant pot bowl and add eggs.

2.   Close the lid of the instant pot and seal it.

3.   Chose the "Steam" program + High Pressure. Cook the eggs for 3 minutes. Make QPR.

4.   Place the eggs in the icy water.

5.   Peel the eggs and cut them into the halves.

6.   Sprinkle the egg halves with the chili powder.

7.   In the shallow bowl mix up cream cheese and chopped jalapeno pepper.

8.   Top the eggs with jalapeno mixture.

Nutritional info per serve: calories 135, fat 9.5, fiber 0.4, carbs 1.3, protein 11.3

Kale Omelet

Prep time: 5 minutes | **Cook time:** 10 minutes |
Yield: 2 servings

Ingredients

2 eggs

1 cup kale, chopped

1 teaspoon heavy cream

2/3 teaspoon white pepper

½ teaspoon butter

Method

1.   Grease the instant pot pan with butter.

2.   Beat the eggs in the separated bowl and whisk them well.

3.   After this, add heavy cream and white pepper. Stir it gently.

4.   Place the chopped kale in the greased pan and add the whisked eggs.

5.   Pour 1 cup of water in the instant pot.

6.   Place the trivet in the instant pot and transfer the egg mixture pan on the trivet.

7.   Close the instant pot and set the "Manual" (High Pressure) program and cook the frittata for 5 minutes. NPR for 5 minutes.

Nutritional info per serve: calories 98, fat 6.3, fiber 0.7, carbs 4.4, protein 6.7

Morning Aromatic Casserole

Prep time: 7 minutes | **Cook time:** 9 minutes |
Yield: 3 servings

Ingredients

3 eggs, beaten

¼ cup coconut cream

¼ teaspoon salt

3 oz Brussel sprouts, chopped

2 oz tomato, chopped

3 oz provolone cheese, shredded

1 teaspoon butter

1 teaspoon smoked paprika

Method

1.   Grease the instant pot pan with the butter.

2.   Put eggs in the bowl, add salt, and smoked paprika. Whisk the eggs well.

3.   After this, add chopped Brussel sprouts and tomato.

4. Pour the mixture into the instant pot pan and sprinkle over with the shredded cheese.

5. Pour 1 cup of the water in the instant pot. Then place the pan with the egg mixture and close the lid.

6. Cook the meal on "Manual" (High pressure) for 4 minutes.

7. Then make naturally release for 5 minutes.

Nutritional info per serve: calories 237, fat 18.2, fiber 2, carbs 5.8, protein 14.5

Breakfast Muffins

Prep time: 5 minutes | **Cook time:** 15 minutes | **Yield:** 2 servings

Ingredients

2 eggs, beaten

¼ cup organic almond milk

2 tablespoons almond flour

¾ teaspoon butter

Method

1. Pour 1 cup of water in the instant pot bowl.

2. Beat the eggs in the bowl and combine together with the almond milk and almond flour.

3. Whisk the mixture.

4. Put the egg mixture in the muffin molds. Add butter.

5. Place the trivet in the instant pot and transfer the muffins in it.

6. Close the instant pot lid and set the "Steam".

7. Cook the muffins for 10 minutes.

8. After this, make the quick release (QPR) for 5 minutes.

Nutritional info per serve: calories 256, fat 21.3, fiber 3, carbs 6.3, protein 12.1

Cups with Greens

Prep time: 6 minutes | **Cook time:** 3 minutes | **Yield:** 2 servings

Ingredients

3 eggs, beaten

¼ cup cauliflower stalks, chopped

2 oz broccoli raab, chopped

1 tablespoon heavy cream

½ teaspoon ground black pepper

¾ teaspoon butter

Method

1. Blend the cauliflower stalk and broccoli raab in the blender until smooth.

2. Mix up together the blended greens and beaten eggs.

3. Add heavy cream, ground black pepper, and butter.

4. Pour the water in the instant pot.

5. After this, pour the egg mixture into the small cups and transfer them in the instant pot.

6. Close the lid and cook on the "Manual" program (High Pressure). Cook the meal for 3 minutes. Make a quick release.

Nutritional info per serve: calories 143, fat 10.8, fiber 0.4, carbs 2.6, protein 9.4

Zucchini Roll

Prep time: 8 minutes | **Cook time:** 12 minutes | **Yield:** 2 servings

Ingredients

½ zucchini, grated

9 oz chicken breast, skinless, boneless

1 tablespoon butter

½ teaspoon white pepper

¼ teaspoon thyme

Method

1. Beat the chicken breast well with the help of the kitchen hammer to get the tender piece.

2. Then sprinkle the chicken breast with the white pepper and thyme.

3. Put the grated zucchini over the chicken breast and flatten it well.

4. Roll up the chicken breast.

5. Wrap the zucchini roll in the foil.

6. Set the instant pot mode "Poultry" and place the zucchini roll in the instant pot bowl.

7. Cook the zucchini roll for 12 minutes. Then make naturally pressure release.

8. Slice the cooked zucchini roll.

Nutritional info per serve: calories 206, fat 9.1, fiber 0.7, carbs 2.1, protein 27.8

Quail Egg Bites

Prep time: 5 minutes | **Cook time:** 7 minutes | **Yield:** 2 servings

Ingredients

6 quail eggs, beaten

1 oz Swiss cheese, grated

½ teaspoon butter

Method

1. Grease the instant pot pan with the butter generously.

2. Then beat the eggs in the bowl and whisk well.

3. Add cheese.

4. Stir the quail eggs gently and transfer into the greased instant pot pan.

5. Place the pan into the instant pot and close the lid.

6. Cook the meal on "Manual" mode (High pressure - QPR) for 4 minutes to get the solid eggs.

7. Cut the cooked quail mixture into bars.

Nutritional info per serve: calories 105, fat 7.9, fiber 0, carbs 0.9, protein 7.4

Omelet "3-Cheese"

Prep time: 5 minutes | **Cook time:** 3 minutes | **Yield:** 2 servings

Ingredients

2 eggs, beaten

1 oz Mozzarella, shredded

¾ teaspoon dried oregano

½ teaspoon coconut oil

1 oz Cheddar cheese, shredded

1 oz Provolone cheese, grated

½ cup water, for cooking

Method

1. Mix up eggs, all cheese, and dried oregano.

2. After this, grease the pan with the coconut and pour the egg mixture inside.

3. Pour ½ cup of water in the instant pot bowl and place the pan with eggs inside.

4. Cook omelet on "Manual" mode for 4 minutes (natural pressure release).

Nutritional info per serve: calories 221, fat 16.5, fiber 0.2, carbs 1.7, protein 16.8

Breakfast Mash

Prep time: 5 minutes | **Cook time:** 7 minutes | **Yield:** 2 servings

Ingredients

¾ cup shredded coconut

2 tablespoons coconut flour

½ cup of coconut milk

1 teaspoon ground flax meal

1 tablespoon Erythritol

1 teaspoon vanilla extract

Method

1.   Mix up together all ingredients and transfer in the instant pot.

2.   Cook the mash on saute mode for 7 minutes. Stir it constantly.

3.   The meal is cooked when it starts to boil.

Nutritional info per serve: calories 285, fat 25.3, fiber 7.2, carbs 13.7, protein 3.5

Cheese Jalapenos

Prep time: 10 minutes | **Cook time:** 5 minutes | **Yield:** 2 servings

Ingredients

2 jalapeno pepper

2 oz Provolone cheese, grated

1 egg, beaten

½ teaspoon ground paprika

1 cup of water

Method

1.   In the mixing bowl, mix up cheese, eggs, and ground paprika.

2.   Then cut the jalapeno peppers into halves and remove the seeds.

3.   Fill the peppers with cheese mixture.

4.   Pour water in the instant pot. Insert the trivet.

5.   Place the jalapenos on the trivet. Close and seal the lid.

6.   Cook the meal on manual mode (high pressure) for 5 minutes. Then make quick pressure release.

Nutritional info per serve: calories 137, fat 9.9, fiber 0.6, carbs 1.9, protein 10.3

Egg Pate

Prep time: 10 minutes | **Cook time:** 5 minutes | **Yield:** 6 servings

Ingredients

8 eggs

1 oz avocado, mashed

2 tablespoons cream cheese

½ teaspoon salt

1 cup water, for cooking

Method

1.   Pour 1 cup of water in the instant pot bowl and add eggs.

2.   Set the "Steam" mode on your instant pot and cook the eggs for 5 minutes (QR).

3.   Meanwhile, mix up cream cheese and mashed avocado.

4.   Peel the cooked eggs and put them in the blender. Blend the eggs until smooth.

5.   Churn together eggs and avocado mash mixture.

6.   The egg pate is cooked.

Nutritional info per serve: calories 105, fat 7.9, fiber 0.3, carbs 1, protein 7.7

Stuffed Lettuce Boats

Prep time: 10 minutes | **Cook time:** 5 minutes | **Yield:** 2 servings

Ingredients

4 oz shrimps

1 tablespoon heavy cream

¾ teaspoon salt

¼ teaspoon dried oregano

4 lettuce leaves

½ teaspoon butter

Method

1.   Peel the shrimps sprinkle with the salt, heavy cream, and dried oregano.

2.   Chop the garlic clove and add in shrimps.

3.   Set the "Stew" mode and put the shrimp mixture inside. Cook the meal for 5 minutes.

4.   Fill the lettuce leaves with cooked shrimps.

Nutritional info per serve: calories 104, fat 4.7, fiber 0.1, carbs 1.5, protein 13.1

Lemon Fish Cakes

Prep time: 15 minutes | **Cook time:** 6 minutes | **Yield:** 2 servings

Ingredients

1 teaspoon butter

½ teaspoon dried thyme

¾ teaspoon garlic powder

10 oz salmon cod fillet

1 oz lemon, sliced

Method

1.   Grind the cod fillet and mix it up with the garlic powder and dried thyme.

2.   Blend the lemon and add it to the fish mixture.

3.   Grease the instant pot pan with the butter.

4.   Make the fish cakes from the mixture and put it in the instant pot.

5.   Cook them on saute mode for 3 minutes from each side or until they are light brown.

Nutritional info per serve: calories 286, fat 18.2, fiber 1.4, carbs 4.3, protein 28.6

Cream Shrimps

Prep time: 5 minutes | **Cook time:** 5 minutes | **Yield:** 2 servings

Ingredients

8 oz shrimps, peeled

½ cup heavy cream

1 teaspoon butter

½ teaspoon chili flakes

Method

1.   Set the "Meat/Stew" mode on the instant pot

2.   Toss butter in the instant pot bowl and add shrimps.

3.   Add all remaining ingredients and close the lid.

4.   Cook the shrimps for 5 minutes on the "Meat/Stew" mode.

Nutritional info per serve: calories 255, fat 14.9, fiber 0, carbs 2.6, protein 26.5

Bacon Kebob

Prep time: 7 minutes | **Cook time:** 10 minutes | **Yield:** 2 servings

Ingredients

1 eggplant

4 bacon slices

1 tablespoon coconut oil

½ teaspoon ground black pepper

Method

1.   Chop the eggplant into the cubes and sprinkle with the coconut oil and ground black pepper.

2.   Wrap the vegetables with bacon and string on the wooden skewers.

3.   Place the kebobs on the trivet and transfer the trivet in the instant pot.

4.   Add ½ cup of water in the instant pot bowl and close the lid.

5.   Cook the meal on "Manual" (High Pressure) mode for 8 minutes. Then make naturally pressure release for 5 minutes.

Nutritional info per serve: calories 323, fat 23.1, fiber 8.2, carbs 14.4, protein 16.4

APPETIZERS AND SIDES

Cheese Chips

Prep time: 10 minutes | **Cook time:** 5 minutes | **Yield:** 4 servings

Ingredients

1 cup cheddar cheese, shredded

1 tablespoon almond flour

Method

1. Mix up cheddar cheese and almond flour.

2. Then preheat the instant pot on saute mode.

3. Line the instant pot bowl with baking paper.

4. After this, make the small rounds from the cheese in the instant pot (on the baking paper) and close the lid.

5. Cook them for 5 minutes on saute mode or until the cheese is melted.

6. Then switch off the instant pot and remove the baking paper with cheese rounds from it.

7. Cool the chips well and remove them from the baking paper.

Nutritional info per serve: calories 154, fat 12.9, fiber 0.8, carbs 1.9, protein 8.5

Cheese Bombs

Prep time: 15 minutes | **Cook time:** 15 minutes | **Yield:** 4 servings

Ingredients

¼ cup Mozzarella, shredded

1 egg, beaten

½ cup almond flour

1 teaspoon butter, softened

1 cup water, for cooking

Method

1. Grease the baking pan with butter.

2. After this, in the mixing bowl mix up Mozzarella, egg, and almond flour.

3. Make the small balls from the mixture and put them in the prepared baking pan.

4. After this, pour water in the instant pot and insert the steamer rack.

5. Place the baking pan with cheese bombs in the instant pot. Close and seal the lid.

6. Cook the meal on manual mode (high pressure) for 15 minutes. Make a quick pressure release.

Nutritional info per serve: calories 49, fat 4.1, fiber 0.4, carbs 0.9, protein 2.6

Zucchini Fries

Prep time: 15 minutes | **Cook time:** 5 minutes | **Yield:** 4 servings

Ingredients

1 zucchini

1 oz Parmesan, grated

1 tablespoon almond flour

½ teaspoon Italian seasonings

1 tablespoon coconut oil

Method

1. Trim the zucchini and cut it into the French fries.

2. Then sprinkle them with grated parmesan, almond flour, and Italian seasonings.

3. Put coconut oil in the instant pot and melt it on saute mode.

4. Put the zucchini in the hot oil in one layer and cook for 2 minutes from each side or until they are golden brown.

5. Dry the zucchini fries with paper towels.

Nutritional info per serve: calories 102, fat 8.7, fiber 1.3, carbs 3.5, protein 4.4

Rangoon Crab Dip

Prep time: 10 minutes | **Cook time:** 3 hours | **Yield:** 3 servings

Ingredients

½ cup Monterey jack cheese, shredded

6 oz crab meat, chopped

½ cup of coconut milk

1 tablespoon scallions, chopped

½ teaspoon garlic powder

1 teaspoon butter, softened

Method

1. Put the crab meat, coconut milk, scallions, and garlic powder in the instant pot.

2. Stir the mixture and add butter.

3. Then top it with cheese and close the lid.

4. Cook the dip on Low for 3 hours.

Nutritional info per serve: calories 226, fat 17.5, fiber 1, carbs 3.9, protein 12.8

Garlic Butter with Herbs

Prep time: 10 minutes | **Cook time:** 8 minutes | **Yield:** 4 servings

Ingredients

1/3 cup butter

1 teaspoon dried parsley

1 tablespoon dried dill

½ teaspoon minced garlic

¼ teaspoon dried thyme

Method

1. Preheat the instant pot on saute mode.

2. Then add butter and melt it.

3. Add dried parsley, dill, minced garlic, and thyme. Stir the butter mixture well.

4. Transfer it in the butter mold and refrigerate until it is solid.

Nutritional info per serve: calories 138, fat 15.4, fiber 0.2, carbs 0.6, protein 0.4

Zucchini and Cheese Scones

Prep time: 15 minutes | **Cook time:** 20 minutes | **Yield:** 4 servings

Ingredients

½ cup zucchini, grated

¼ cup Cheddar cheese, shredded

1 egg, beaten

¼ cup coconut flour

½ teaspoon ground black pepper

1 cup water, for cooking

Method

1. Make the dough: mix up zucchini, cheese, egg, coconut flour, and ground black pepper.

2. Then transfer the mixture in the non-stick baking pan and flatten well.

3. Pour water and insert the rack in the instant pot.

4. Put the pan with zucchini mixture on the rack. Close and seal the lid.

5. Cook the meal on manual mode (high pressure) for 20 minutes.

6. Make a quick pressure release.

7. Cool the cooked zucchini meal well and cut into the scones.

Nutritional info per serve: calories 71, fat 3.7, fiber 3.5, carbs 6.2, protein 3.9

Flax Meal Bread

Prep time: 20 minutes | **Cook time:** 20 minutes | **Yield:** 4 servings

Ingredients

1 egg, beaten

2 tablespoons cream cheese

½ cup coconut flour

3 tablespoons flax meal

¼ teaspoon baking powder

1 teaspoon lemon juice

1 teaspoon butter

1 cup water, for cooking

Method

1. Mix up egg, cream cheese, coconut flour, flax meal, baking powder, lemon juice, and knead the dough.

2. Then grease the bread mold with butter and transfer the dough inside.

3. Flatten it in the shape of the bread.

4. Then pour water in the instant pot and insert the bread mold.

5. Close and seal the lid.

6. Cook the bread on manual mode (high pressure) for 20 minutes and then do the quick pressure release.

7. Cool the bread to the room temperature and slice it.

Nutritional info per serve: calories 135, fat 8.2, fiber 7.5, carbs 10.9, protein 5.9

Zucchini Ravioli

Prep time: 15 minutes | **Cook time:** 20 minutes | **Yield:** 2 servings

Ingredients

1 zucchini, trimmed

1 tablespoon ricotta cheese

2 oz spinach, chopped

1 teaspoon olive oil

1 garlic clove, minced

¼ cup keto marinara sauce

¼ cup chicken broth

Method

1. Slice the zucchini into vertical slices with the help of the potato peeler.

2. Then heat up olive oil on saute mode for 1 minute.

3. Add spinach and garlic. Cook it for 3 minutes and transfer in the bowl.

4. Add ricotta cheese.

5. Make the cross from 4 zucchini slices and put the small amount of the ricotta cheese mixture inside. Wrap the zucchini into the balls and place them in the instant pot in one layer.

6. Add chicken broth and marinara sauce.

7. Close the lid and saute the meal for 15 minutes on saute mode.

Nutritional info per serve: calories 87, fat 4.3, fiber 2.5, carbs 9.6, protein 4.2

Eggplant Parm

Prep time: 15 minutes | **Cook time:** 10 minutes | **Yield:** 2 servings

Ingredients

1 eggplant, sliced

1 teaspoon dried basil

1/3 cup keto marinara sauce

¼ cup Mozzarella, shredded

1 tablespoon butter

½ cup beef broth

Method

1.   Grease the instant pot bowl with butter.

2.   Then place the layer of the sliced eggplants in the instant pot and sprinkle it with shredded cheese and dried basil.

3.   Repeat the step one more time.

4.   Add beef broth and keto marinara sauce.

5.   Close and seal the lid and cook the eggplant parm for 10 minutes.

6.   Make a quick pressure release and cool the meal for 5 minutes before serving.

Nutritional info per serve: calories 140, fat 7.7, fiber 8.4, carbs 15.5, protein 4.5

Cheese and Mushrooms Cakes

Prep time: 15 minutes | **Cook time:** 10 minutes | **Yield:** 3 servings

Ingredients

7 oz white mushrooms, grinded

1 teaspoon butter

1/3 teaspoon salt

1 egg, beaten

¾ teaspoon chili pepper

3 oz Cheddar cheese, shredded

Method

1.   Mix up all the ingredients together, except the butter.

2.   Heat up butter on saute mode.

3.   Then make the small cakes from the mushroom mixture and put them in the hot butter.

4.   Cook the meal on saute mode for 4 minutes from each side.

Nutritional info per serve: calories 161, fat 12.3, fiber 0.7, carbs 2.8, protein 11

Cream Cheese Puree

Prep time: 8 minutes | **Cook time:** 5 minutes | **Yield:** 2 servings

Ingredients

1 cup of water

½ teaspoon salt

2 tablespoons cream cheese

10 oz cauliflower, chopped

Method

1.   Place the chopped cauliflower in the instant pot.

2.   Add salt and water.

3.   Set the "Manual" mode (High pressure) on the instant pot.

4.   Set the timer for 5 minutes.

5.   When the time is over – use the quick pressure release method.

6.   Transfer the cauliflower (without liquid) in the blender. Blend it until smooth.

7.   After this, transfer the cauliflower mash in the bowl. Add cream cheese and stir the puree until homogenous.

Nutritional info per serve: calories 70, fat 3.6, fiber 3.5, carbs 7.8, protein 3.6

Butter Zoodles

Prep time: 15 minutes | **Cook time:** 10 minutes | **Yield:** 2 servings

Ingredients

1 cup of water

1 large zucchini

2 tablespoons butter, softened

Method

1.   Make the zoodles from zucchini with the help of the spiralizer.

2.   Then pour water in the instant pot and bring it to boil on saute mode.

3.   Then add zucchini zoodles and let them cook for 1 minute.

4.   Remove the zoodles from water and add butter. Stir well.

Nutritional info per serve: calories 128, fat 11.8, fiber 1.8, carbs 5.4, protein 2.1

Chili Zoodles

Prep time: 7 minutes | **Cook time:** 3 minutes | **Yield:** 2 servings

Ingredients

1 teaspoon chili flakes

2 zucchini

½ cup chicken stock

1 teaspoon coconut oil

Method

1.   Make the noodles from the zucchini with the help of the spiralizer.

2.   Sprinkle zucchini noodles with the salt and chili flakes.

3.   Place the chicken stock and coconut oil in the instant pot bowl and preheat the liquid on the "Saute" mode.

4.   Add the spiralized zucchini and cook on "Manual" mode - Zero –QPR.

5.   The meal is cooked.

Nutritional info per serve: calories 54, fat 2.8, fiber 2.2, carbs 6.8, protein 2.6

Cremini Mushrooms Stew

Prep time: 8 minutes | **Cook time:** 25 minutes | **Yield:** 2 servings

Ingredients

2 teaspoons butter

1 cup cremini mushrooms, sliced

½ cup heavy cream

½ teaspoon white pepper

¼ teaspoon turmeric

Method

1.   Melt the butter in the instant pot bowl on the "Saute" mode.

2.   Add heavy cream, white pepper, turmeric, and stir well.

3.   Preheat the liquid until it starts to boil.

4.   Add sliced mushrooms and stir well.

5.   After this, close the lid and cook the saute on the "Saute" mode for 20 minutes. Reduce the time of cooking if you want the solid texture of the mushrooms.

Nutritional info per serve: calories 149, fat 15, fiber 0.4, carbs 2.8, protein 1.60

Tender Celery Cubes

Prep time: 6 minutes | **Cook time:** 15 minutes | **Yield:** 2 servings

Ingredients

1 cup celery root, chopped

1 garlic clove, chopped

½ teaspoon ground coriander

½ teaspoon salt

¾ teaspoon ground cinnamon

½ cup of coconut milk

1 teaspoon butter

Method

1.   Put all ingredients in the instant pot.

2.   Close and seal the lid.

3.   Cook the ragout on the "Saute" mode for 15 minutes to get the soft vegetable texture.

Nutritional info per serve: calories 192, fat 16.5, fiber 3.2, carbs 11.7, protein 2.7

Sauteed Green Mix

Prep time: 5 minutes | **Cook time:** 10 minutes | **Yield:** 2 servings

Ingredients

2 cups spinach, chopped

1 cup kale, chopped

½ cup chicken stock

1 teaspoon cream cheese

½ teaspoon salt

½ cup broccoli raab, chopped

Method

1.   Pour the chicken stock in the instant pot bowl.

2.   Add cream cheese, salt, spinach, kale, and broccoli raab.

3.   Cook the meal on the "Saute" mode for 5 minutes. Stir well.

4.   Discard the greens from the chicken stock gravy and transfer on the plates.

Nutritional info per serve: calories 37, fat 0.8, fiber 1.2, carbs 5.6, protein 2.7

Garlic Asparagus

Prep time: 6 minutes | **Cook time:** 4 minutes | **Yield:** 2 servings

Ingredients

9 oz asparagus

½ teaspoon garlic powder

1 teaspoon butter

¾ teaspoon minced garlic

2 oz Parmesan, shredded

1 cup water, for cooking

Method

1.   Grease the springform pan with butter.

2.   Place the asparagus in the springform pan.

3.   Sprinkle the vegetables with the garlic powder, and minced garlic.

4.   Add water in the instant pot. Insert the springform with asparagus inside.

5.   Close the lid and set the "Manual" mode (High pressure) for 4 minutes.

6.   When the asparagus is cooked – make quick pressure release.

7.   Transfer the asparagus on the serving plates immediately and sprinkle with the shredded cheese.

Nutritional info per serve: calories 137, fat 8.2, fiber 2.8, carbs 6.8, protein 12.1

Marjoram Cauliflower Florets

Prep time: 5 minutes | **Cook time:** 1 minute |
Yield: 2 servings

Ingredients

1 teaspoon butter

½ teaspoon salt

1 teaspoon dried marjoram

½ cup beef broth

10 oz cauliflower

Method

1.   Cut the cauliflower into the florets and sprinkle with the dried marjoram and salt.

2.   Transfer the vegetables in the instant pot.

3.   Add butter and beef broth.

4.   Close the lid and set "Manual" mode (High pressure); cook the meal for 1 minute.

5.   Then make quick pressure release and open the lid.

6.   Add the butter in the cauliflower.

Nutritional info per serve: calories 63, fat 2.4, fiber 3.7, carbs 7.9, protein 4.1

Cream Keto Beans

Prep time: 5 minutes | **Cook time:** 3 minutes |
Yield: 4 servings

Ingredients

2 teaspoons butter

11 oz green beans

1 cup coconut cream

Method

1.   Put all ingredients in the instant pot

2.   Set the "Manual" mode (High pressure) and put time for 2 minutes.

3.   When the time is over – make quick pressure release.

Nutritional info per serve: calories 179, fat 16.3, fiber 4, carbs 8.9, protein 2.8

Ginger Cabbage

Prep time: 7 minutes | **Cook time:** 15 minutes |
Yield: 2 servings

Ingredients

½ tablespoon ginger paste

10 oz white cabbage, shredded

1 teaspoon butter

½ cup heavy cream

½ teaspoon salt

Method

1.   Place the cabbage in the big mixing bowl.

2.   Sprinkle the cabbage with the ginger paste and salt.

3.   Melt the butter on the "Saute" mode in the instant pot.

4.   Then add all the shredded cabbage and heavy cream.

5.   Set the "steam" mode and cook the cabbage for 10 minutes.

6.   Transfer the cooked meal on the serving plates and enjoy!

Nutritional info per serve: calories 160, fat 13.2, fiber 3.7, carbs 10, protein 2.6

Aromatic Eggplant Mix

Prep time: 5 minutes | **Cook time:** 30 minutes | **Yield:** 2 servings

Ingredients

8 oz eggplant, chopped

3 oz asparagus, chopped

1 teaspoon salt

1 teaspoon ground cumin

1 cup chicken broth

1 bell pepper, chopped

Method

1. Put all vegetables in the instant pot.

2. Close the lid and cook the meal on saute mode for 30 minutes.

3. When the time is finished and the meal is cooked, stir it well with the help of the spoon.

Nutritional info per serve: calories 186, fat 12.1, fiber 4.9, carbs 11.2, protein 10.8

Italian Style Kale

Prep time: 5 minutes | **Cook time:** 3 minutes | **Yield:** 3 servings

Ingredients

10 oz kale, Italian dark-leaf

1 tablespoon Italian seasonings

1 cup water, for cooking

Method

1. Chop the kale roughly and put it in the steamer pan. Sprinkle the greens with seasonings and stir well.

2. Then pour water and insert the steamer rack in the instant pot.

3. Put the pan with kale in the instant pot.

4. Cook the meal on the "Steam" mode for 3 minutes.

Nutritional info per serve: calories 61, fat 1.4, fiber 1.4, carbs 10.4, protein 2.8

Sesame Bok Choy

Prep time: 5 minutes | **Cook time:** 7 minutes | **Yield:** 2 servings

Ingredients

2 cups bok choy, sliced

1 teaspoon sesame seeds

1 tablespoon apple cider vinegar

1 teaspoon sesame oil

¾ teaspoon salt

1 cup water, for cooking

Method

1. Pour water and insert the steamer rack in the instant pot.

2. Put the bok choy in the steamer rack and close the lid.

3. Cook the vegetables on the "Steam" mode for 3 minutes.

4. Make a quick pressure release and transfer the bok choy on the plate.

5. Sprinkle the meal with salt, sesame oil, apple cider vinegar, and sesame seeds.

6. Shake the bok choy gently.

7. Serve the bok choy warm!

Nutritional info per serve: calories 35, fat 2.9, fiber 0.7, carbs 1.8, protein 1.3

Kale Saute with Flax Seeds

Prep time: 5 minutes | **Cook time:** 4 minutes | **Yield:** 2 servings

Ingredients

1 cup Kale, Italian dark-leaf, chopped

1 teaspoon butter

1 tablespoon flax seeds

¾ teaspoon ground nutmeg

1 teaspoon olive oil

¼ cup of water

Method

1. Toss butter in the instant pot bowl and melt it on the "Saute" mode.

2. Add the chopped kale. Sprinkle the kale leaves with the salt and ground nutmeg.

3. Add water Stir the kale well.

4. Cook it on the "Saute" mode for 4 minutes.

5. Then transfer the cooked kale on the serving plates and sprinkle with the olive oil and flax seeds.

Nutritional info per serve: calories 76, fat 5.4, fiber 1.6, carbs 4.9, protein 1.7

Brussel Sprouts Hash

Prep time: 6 minutes | **Cook time:** 9 minutes | **Yield:** 2 servings

Ingredients

1 cup Brussel sprouts, chopped

1 egg, beaten

2 oz Parmesan cheese, shredded

1 tablespoon butter, melted

Method

1. Combine together the chopped Brussel sprouts and beaten egg. Stir the mixture until homogenous.

2. Add shredded cheese and butter.

3. Stir the mixture with the help of a spatula.

4. After this, transfer the mixture in the non-sticky springform pan or cake mold.

5. Pour water in the instant pot.

6. Place the pan in the instant pot.

7. Lock the instant pot lid and seal it.

8. Set the "Manual" mode – High Pressure.

9. Cook hash brown for 4 minutes. Then make naturally pressure release for 5 minutes.

Nutritional info per serve: calories 192, fat 14.2, fiber 1.7, carbs 5.2, protein 13.4

Tender Purple Petals

Prep time: 10 minutes | **Cook time:** 5 minutes | **Yield:** 2 servings

Ingredients

7 oz purple cabbage

¼ teaspoon salt

1 teaspoon butter

½ cup chicken broth

Method

1. Cut the cabbage into the petals and sprinkle with salt.

2. Place the cabbage into the instant pot.

3. Add butter and chicken broth.

4. Close the lid and set the "Steam" mode 5 minutes. Then make quick pressure release.

Nutritional info per serve: calories 51, fat 2.4, fiber 2.5, carbs 6, protein 2.5

Lemon Flavored Broccoli

Prep time: 10 minutes | **Cook time:** 18 minutes | **Yield:** 2 servings

Ingredients

1 teaspoon salt

8 oz broccoli

¾ cup cream cheese

¼ cup of water

1 teaspoon grated lemon

Method

1. Cut the broccoli into the medium pieces and place them in the instant pot.

2. Add cream cheese and start to saute it for 3 minutes on the "Saute" mode.

3. Then add salt and grated lemon.

4. Stir gently and close the lead. Cook the meal on "Saute mode" for 15 minutes.

5. Serve the broccoli with a small amount of gravy.

Nutritional info per serve: calories 343, fat 30.7, fiber 3, carbs 10.1, protein 9.8

Celery Stalk Chicken Salad

Prep time: 10- minutes | **Cook time:** 15 minutes | **Yield:** 2 servings

Ingredients

7 oz celery stalks, chopped

4 oz chicken fillet

1 teaspoon ground black pepper

½ teaspoon salt

1 cup of water

Method

1. Put the chicken in the instant pot. Add water and ground black pepper.

2. Cook the chicken on manual mode (high pressure) for 15 minutes + QPR.

3. Then shred the chicken and mix it up with salt and chopped celery stalk.

Nutritional info per serve: calories 144, fat 6.1, fiber 1.9, carbs 3.8, protein 17.6

Parsley Fennel

Prep time: 10 minutes | **Cook time:** 5 minutes | **Yield:** 2 servings

Ingredients

1 fennel bulb, sliced

¾ cup fresh parsley, chopped

1 cup of water

1 teaspoon apple cider vinegar

1 tablespoon coconut aminos

1 tablespoon olive oil

Method

1. Pour water and insert the steamer rack in the instant pot.

2. Put the sliced fennel inside and cook it on Steam mode for 5 minutes.

3. Then transfer the fennel in the big bowl and sprinkle with apple cider vinegar, parsley, and olive oil.

4. Shake the fenne gently.

Nutritional info per serve: calories 112, fat 7.4, fiber 4.4, carbs 11.5, protein 2.1

Turmeric Cauliflower Shred

Prep time: 5 minutes | **Cook time:** 5 minutes |
Yield: 2 servings

Ingredients

½ cup chicken broth

8 oz cauliflower, shredded

1 teaspoon butter

1 teaspoon ground turmeric

Method

1. Put the butter in the instant pot and preheat it on the "Saute" mode.

2. Add shredded cauliflower and salt. Stir the mixture and cook for 1 minute more.

3. After this, add chicken broth and turmeric, mix up the ingredients and lock the instant pot.

4. Set the "Manual" mode (High pressure) and cook the side dish for 1 minute.

5. After this, make a quick pressure release (follow the directions of your instant pot).

Nutritional info per serve: calories 59, fat 2.5, fiber 3.1, carbs 7, protein 3.6

Butter Konjac Noodles

Prep time: 10 minutes | **Cook time:** 1 minute |
Yield: 2 servings

Ingredients

7 oz Konjac Noodles

1 teaspoon butter, melted

1 cup of water

Method

1. Pour water in the instant pot and bring it to boil on Saute mode.

2. Add konjac noodles and leave them in the water for 1 minute.

3. Then rinse the noodles and carefully mix them up with butter.

Nutritional info per serve: calories 26, fat 11.9, fiber 3, carbs 3.5, protein 0

Broccoli Puree

Prep time: 10 minutes | **Cook time:** 6 minutes |
Yield: 2 servings

Ingredients

7 oz broccoli, chopped

½ cup heavy cream

Method

1. Pour heavy cream in the instant pot.

2. Add broccoli and close the lid.

3. Cook the vegetables on manual mode (high pressure) for 6 minutes of +quick pressure release.

4. Transfer the broccoli and ¼ part of all liquid in the blender and blend the mixture until you get a smooth puree.

Nutritional info per serve: calories 137, fat 11.4, fiber 2.6, carbs 7.4, protein 3.4

Salmon Salad with Feta

Prep time: 10 minutes | **Cook time:** 4 minutes |
Yield: 2 servings

Ingredients

2 oz Feta, crumbled

6 oz salmon

1 cup lettuce, chopped

1 teaspoon olive oil

½ teaspoon salt

1 cup water, for cooking

Method

1.   Sprinkle the salmon with salt and wrap in foil.

2.   Place the salmon on the trivet and transfer it in the instant pot bowl.

3.   Add 1 cup of water in the instant pot bowl and close the lid.

4.   Cook the salmon on "Manual" mode (High Pressure) for 4 minutes (QR).

5.   Meanwhile, tear the lettuce and toss it in the salad bowl.

6.   Sprinkle it with olive oil.

7.   When the salmon is cooked, chop it roughly and add in the lettuce.

8.   Add crumbled Feta and shake the salad.

Nutritional info per serve: calories 211, fat 13.7, fiber 0.2, carbs 2, protein 20.7

Scrambled Eggs Salad

Prep time: 10 minutes | **Cook time:** 5 minutes | **Yield:** 2 servings

Ingredients

1 tomato, chopped

2 eggs

2 tablespoons coconut milk

1 teaspoon butter

1 bell pepper, chopped

Method

1.   Heat up butte on saute mode.

2.   Crack the eggs in the butter.

3.   Add coconut milk and stir the egg mixture until smooth. Saute it for 2 minutes and then scramble again. Cook the eggs for 2 minutes more and transfer in the bowl.

4.   Add tomato and bell pepper.

5.   Mix up the salad.

Nutritional info per serve: calories 139, fat 10.1, fiber 1.5, carbs 6.9, protein 6.8

Zucchini Cheese Rings

Prep time: 15 minutes | **Cook time:** 3 minutes | **Yield:** 2 servings

Ingredients

1 zucchini

1 cup cheddar cheese, shredded

2 teaspoon butter, softened

2 cup of water

Method

1.   Cut the zucchini into rings and remove the center of every ring.

2.   Then grease the baking pan with softened butter and place the zucchini inside in one layer.

3.   Fill every vegetable ring with shredded cheese.

4.   After this, pour water and insert the trivet in the instant pot.

5.   Put the baking pan with zucchini rings on the trivet.

6.   Close and seal the lid.

7.   Cook the meal on manual mode (high pressure) for 3 minutes. Then make a quick pressure release.

8.   Cool the zucchini rings for 5-7 minutes before serving.

Nutritional info per serve: calories 277, fat 22.7, fiber 1.1, carbs 4, protein 15.3

SOUP AND STEWS

Tomatillos Fish Stew

Prep time: 15 minutes | **Cook time:** 12 minutes | **Yield:** 2 servings

Ingredients

2 tomatillos, chopped

10 oz salmon fillet, chopped

1 teaspoon ground paprika

½ teaspoon ground turmeric

1 cup coconut cream

½ teaspoon salt

Method

1. Put all ingredients in the instant pot.

2. Close and seal the lid.

3. Cook the fish stew on manual mode (high pressure) for 12 minutes.

4. Then allow the natural pressure release for 10 minutes.

Nutritional info per serve: calories 479, fat 37.9, fiber 3.8, carbs 9.6, protein 30.8

Chili Verde Soup

Prep time: 10 minutes | **Cook time:** 25 minutes | **Yield:** 4 servings

Ingredients

2 oz chili Verde sauce

½ cup Cheddar cheese, shredded

5 cups chicken broth

1-pound chicken breast, skinless, boneless

1 tablespoon dried cilantro

Method

1. Put chicken breast and chicken broth in the instant pot.

2. Add cilantro, close and seal the lid.

3. Then cook the ingredients on manual (high pressure) for 15 minutes.

4. Make a quick pressure release and open the li.

5. Shred the chicken breast with the help of the fork.

6. Add dried cilantro and chili Verde sauce in the soup and cook it on saute mode for 10 minutes.

7. Then add dried cilantro and stir well.

Nutritional info per serve: calories 257, fat 10.2, fiber 0.2, carbs 4, protein 34.5

Pepper Stuffing Soup

Prep time: 10 minutes | **Cook time:** 14 minutes | **Yield:** 4 servings

Ingredients

1 cup ground beef

½ cup cauliflower, shredded

1 teaspoon dried oregano

½ teaspoon salt

1 teaspoon tomato paste

1 teaspoon minced garlic

4 cups of water

¼ cup of coconut milk

Method

1. Put all ingredients in the instant pot bowl and stir well.

2. Then close and seal the lid.

3. Cook the soup on manual mode (high pressure) for 14 minutes.

4. When the time of cooking is finished, make a quick pressure release and open the lid.

Nutritional info per serve: calories 106, fat 7.7, fiber 0.9, carbs 2.2, protein 7.3

Steak Soup

Prep time: 10 minutes | **Cook time:** 40 minutes | **Yield:** 5 servings

Ingredients

5 oz scallions, diced

1 tablespoon coconut oil

1 oz daikon, diced

1-pound beef round steak, chopped

1 teaspoon dried thyme

5 cups of water

½ teaspoon ground black pepper

Method

1. Heat up coconut oil on saute mode for 2 minutes.

2. Add daikon and scallions.

3. After this, stir them well and add chopped beef steak, thyme, and ground black pepper.

4. Saute the ingredients for 5 minutes more and then add water.

5. Close and seal the lid.

6. Cook the soup on manual mode (high pressure) for 35 minutes. Make a quick pressure release.

Nutritional info per serve: calories 232, fat 11, fiber 0.9, carbs 2.5, protein 29.5

Meat Spinach Stew

Prep time: 20 minutes | **Cook time:** 30 minutes | **Yield:** 4 servings

Ingredients

2 cups spinach, chopped

1-pound beef sirloin, chopped

1 teaspoon allspices

3 cups chicken broth

1 cup of coconut milk

1 teaspoon coconut aminos

Method

1. Put all ingredients in the instant pot.

2. Close and seal the lid.

3. After this, set the manual mode (high pressure) and cook the stew for 30 minutes.

4. When the cooking time is finished, allow the natural pressure release for 10 minutes.

5. Stir the stew gently before serving.

Nutritional info per serve: calories 383, fat 22.2, fiber 1.8, carbs 5.1, protein 39.9

Leek Soup

Prep time: 10 minutes | **Cook time:** 15 minutes | **Yield:** 4 servings

Ingredients

7 oz leek, chopped

2 oz Monterey Jack cheese, shredded

1 teaspoon Italian seasonings

½ teaspoon salt

4 tablespoons butter

2 cups chicken broth

Method

1. Heat up butter in the instant pot for 4 minutes.

2. Then add chopped leek, salt, and Italian seasonings.

3. Cook the leek on saute mode for 5 minutes. Stir the vegetables from time to time.

4. After this, add chicken broth and close the lid.

5. Cook the soup on saute mode for 10 minutes.

6. Then add shredded cheese and stir it till the cheese is melted.

7. The soup is cooked.

Nutritional info per serve: calories 208, fat 17, fiber 0.9, carbs 7.7, protein 6.8

Asparagus Soup

Prep time: 10 minutes | **Cook time:** 17 minutes | **Yield:** 4 servings

Ingredients

1 cup asparagus, chopped

2 cups of coconut milk

1 teaspoon salt

½ teaspoon cayenne pepper

3 oz scallions, diced

1 teaspoon olive oil

Method

1. Saute the chopped asparagus, scallions, and olive oil in the instant pot for 7 minutes.

2. Then stir the vegetables well and add cayenne pepper, salt, and coconut milk

3. Cook the soup on manual mode (high pressure) for 10 minutes.

4. After this, make a quick pressure release and open the lid.

5. Blend the soup until you get the creamy texture.

Nutritional info per serve: calories 300, fat 29.9, fiber 4, carbs 9.6, protein 3.9

Bok Choy Soup

Prep time: 5 minutes | **Cook time:** 2 minutes | **Yield:** 1 serving

Ingredients

1 bok choy stalk, chopped

¼ teaspoon nutritional yeast

½ teaspoon onion powder

¼ teaspoon chili flakes

1 cup chicken broth

Method

1. Put all ingredients from the list above in the instant pot.

2. Close and seal the lid and cook the soup on manual (high pressure) for 2 minutes.

3. Make a quick pressure release.

Nutritional info per serve: calories 58 fat 1.7, fiber 1.3, carbs 4.5, protein 6.9

Curry Kale Soup

Prep time: 10 minutes | **Cook time:** 15 minutes | **Yield:** 3 servings

Ingredients

2 cups kale

1 tablespoon fresh cilantro

1 teaspoon curry paste

½ cup heavy cream

½ cup ground chicken

1 teaspoon almond butter

½ teaspoon salt

1 cup chicken stock

Method

1.   Blend the kale until smooth and put it in the instant pot.

2.   Add cilantro, almond butter, and ground chicken. Saute the mixture for 5 minutes.

3.   Meanwhile, in the shallow bowl, mix up curry paste and heavy cream. When the liquid is smooth, pour it in the instant pot.

4.   Add chicken stock and salt, and close the lid.

5.   Cook the soup on manual (high pressure) for 10 minutes. Make a quick pressure release.

Nutritional info per serve: calories 183, fat 13.3, fiber 1.2, carbs 7, protein 9.9

Turmeric Rutabaga Soup

Prep time: 15 minutes | **Cook time:** 15 minutes | **Yield:** 5 servings

Ingredients

3 turnips, chopped

1 teaspoon ginger paste

2 oz celery, chopped

1 teaspoon ground turmeric

1 teaspoon minced garlic

2 cups of coconut milk

1 cup beef broth

2 oz bell pepper, chopped

Method

1.   Place all ingredients in the instant pot and stir them gently.

2.   Then close and seal the lid; set manual mode (high pressure) and cook the soup for 15 minutes.

3.   Then allow the natural pressure release for 10 minutes and ladle the soup into the serving bowls.

Nutritional info per serve: calories 255, fat 23.2, fiber 3.6, carbs 11.4, protein 4

Cream of Mushrooms Soup

Prep time: 10 minutes | **Cook time:** 35 minutes | **Yield:** 6 servings

Ingredients

3 cups cremini mushrooms, sliced

1 cup of coconut milk

1 tablespoon almond flour

1 teaspoon salt

1 teaspoon ground black pepper

4 cups chicken broth

3 tablespoons butter

Method

1.   Melt the butter on saute mode.

2.   Add cremini mushrooms and saute them for 10 minutes. Stir them with the help of the spatula from time to time.

3.   After this, in the bowl mix up salt, almond flour, and ground black pepper. Add coconut milk and stir the liquid.

4.   Pour the liquid over the mushrooms.

5.   Add chicken broth. Close and seal the lid.

6.   Cook the soup on saute mode for 25 minutes.

Nutritional info per serve: calories 206, fat 18.6, fiber 1.7, carbs 5.5, protein 6.2

Flu Soup

Prep time: 10 minutes | **Cook time:** 15 minutes | **Yield:** 4 servings

Ingredients

1 cup mushrooms, chopped

1 cup spinach, chopped

3 oz scallions, diced

2 oz Cheddar cheese, shredded

1 teaspoon cayenne pepper

1 cup organic almond milk

2 cups chicken broth

½ teaspoon salt

Method

1.   Put all ingredients in the instant pot and close the lid.

2.   Set the manual mode (high pressure) and cook the soup for 15 minutes.

3.   Make a quick pressure release.

4.   Blend the soup with the help of the immersion blender.

5.   When the soup will get smooth texture – it is cooked.

Nutritional info per serve: calories 228, fat 19.9, fiber 2.3, carbs 6.6, protein 8.5

Jalapeno Soup

Prep time: 10 minutes | **Cook time:** 10 minutes | **Yield:** 4 servings

Ingredients

2 jalapeno peppers, sliced

3 oz pancetta, chopped

½ cup heavy cream

2 cups of water

½ cup Monterey jack cheese, shredded

½ teaspoon garlic powder

1 teaspoon coconut oil

½ teaspoon smoked paprika

Method

1.   Toss pancetta in the instant pot, add coconut oil and cook it for 4 minutes on saute mode. Stir it from time to time.

2.   After this, add sliced jalapenos, garlic powder, and smoked paprika.

3.   Stir the ingredients for 1 minute.

4.   Add heavy cream and water.

5.   Then add Monterey Jack cheese and stir the soup well.

6.   Close and seal the lid; cook the soup for 5 minutes on manual mode (high pressure); make a quick pressure release.

Nutritional info per serve: calories 234, fat 20, fiber 0.4, carbs 1.7, protein 11.8

Garden Soup

Prep time: 20 minutes | **Cook time:** 29 minutes | **Yield:** 5 servings

Ingredients

½ cup cauliflower florets

1 cup kale, chopped

1 garlic clove, diced

1 tablespoon olive oil

1 1 teaspoon sea salt

6 cups beef broth

2 tablespoons chives, chopped

Method

1. Heat up olive oil in the instant pot on saute mode for 2 minutes and add clove.

2. Cook the vegetables for 2 minutes and stir well.

3. Add kale, cauliflower, sea salt, chives, and beef broth.

4. Close and seal the lid.

5. Cook the soup on manual mode (high pressure) for 5 minutes.

6. Then make a quick pressure release and open the lid.

7. Ladle the soup into the bowls.

Nutritional info per serve: calories 80, fat 4.5, fiber 0.5, carbs 2.3, protein 6.5

Shirataki Noodle Soup

Prep time: 25 minutes | **Cook time:** 15 minutes | **Yield:** 2 servings

Ingredients

2 oz shirataki noodles

2 cups of water

6 oz chicken fillet, chopped

1 teaspoon salt

1 tablespoon coconut aminos

Method

1. Pour water in the instant pot bowl.

2. Add salt and chopped chicken fillet. Close and seal the lid.

3. Cook the ingredients on manual mode (high pressure) for 15 minutes. Allow the natural pressure release for 10 minutes.

4. After this, add shirataki noodles and coconut aminos.

5. Leave the soup for 10 minutes to rest.

Nutritional info per serve: calories 175, fat 6.3, fiber 3, carbs 1.5, protein 24.8

Cordon Blue Soup

Prep time: 15 minutes | **Cook time:** 6 minutes | **Yield:** 4 servings

Ingredients

4 cups chicken broth

7 oz ham, chopped

3 oz Mozzarella cheese, shredded

1 teaspoon ground black pepper

½ teaspoon salt

2 tablespoons ricotta cheese

2 oz scallions, chopped

Method

1. Put all ingredients in the instant pot bowl and stir gently.

2. Close and seal the lid; cook the soup on manual mode (high pressure) for 6 minutes.

3. Then allow the natural pressure release for 10 minutes and ladle the soup into the bowls.

Nutritional info per serve: calories 196, fat 10.1, fiber 1.2, carbs 5.3, protein 20.3

Bacon Soup

Prep time: 10 minutes | **Cook time:** 20 minutes | **Yield:** 4 servings

Ingredients

3 oz bacon, chopped

1 cup cheddar cheese, shredded

1 tablespoon scallions, chopped

3 cups beef broth

1 cup of coconut milk

1 teaspoon curry powder

Method

1.   Heat up the instant pot on saute mode for 3 minutes and add bacon.

2.   Cook it for 5 minutes. Stir it from time to time.

3.   Then add scallions and curry powder. Cook the ingredients for 5 minutes more. Stir them from time to time.

4.   After this, add coconut milk and beef broth.

5.   Add cheddar cheese and stir the soup well.

6.   Cook it on manual mode (high pressure) for 10 minutes. Make a quick pressure release.

7.   Mix up the soup well before serving.

Nutritional info per serve: calories 398, fat 33.6, fiber 1.5, carbs 5.1, protein 20

Paprika Zucchini Soup

Prep time: 10 minutes | **Cook time:** 1 minute | **Yield:** 2 servings

Ingredients

1 zucchini, grated

1 teaspoon ground paprika

½ teaspoon cayenne pepper

½ cup of coconut milk

1 cup beef broth

1 tablespoon dried cilantro

1 oz Parmesan, grated

Method

1.   Put the grated zucchini, paprika, cayenne pepper, coconut milk, beef broth, and dried cilantro in the instant pot.

2.   Close and seal the lid.

3.   Cook the soup on manual (high pressure) for 1 minute. Make a quick pressure release.

4.   Ladle the soup in the serving bowls and top with parmesan.

Nutritional info per serve: calories 223, fat 18.4, fiber 2.9, carbs 8.4, protein 9.7

Egg Drop Soup

Prep time: 5 minutes | **Cook time:** 10 minutes | **Yield:** 4 servings

Ingredients

4 cups chicken broth

2 tablespoons fresh dill, chopped

2 eggs, beaten

1 teaspoon salt

Method

1.   Pour chicken broth in the instant pot.

2.   Add salt and bring it to boil on Saute mode.

3.   Then add beaten eggs and stir the liquid well.

4.   Add dill and saute it for 5 minutes.

5.   The soup is cooked.

Nutritional info per serve: calories 74, fat 3.6, fiber 0.2, carbs 2, protein 7.9

Buffalo Style Soup

Prep time: 7 minutes | **Cook time:** 10 minutes | **Yield:** 2 servings

Ingredients

6 oz chicken, cooked

2 oz Mozzarella, shredded

4 tablespoons coconut milk

¼ teaspoon white pepper

¾ teaspoon salt

2 tablespoons keto Buffalo sauce

1 oz celery stalk, chopped

1 cup of water

Method

1. Place the chopped celery stalk, water, salt, white pepper, coconut milk, and Mozzarella in the instant pot. Stir it gently.

2. Set the "Manual" mode (High pressure) and turn on the timer for 7 minutes.

3. Shred the cooked chicken and combine it together with Buffalo Sauce.

4. Make quick pressure release and transfer the soup on the bowls.

5. Add shredded chicken and stir it.

Nutritional info per serve: calories 287, fat 14.8, fiber 1.5, carbs 4.3, protein 33.5

Vegan Cream Soup

Prep time: 5 minutes | **Cook time:** 8 minutes | **Yield:** 2 servings

Ingredients

1 cup of coconut milk

1 teaspoon coconut oil

½ teaspoon paprika

2 cups cauliflower, chopped

1 teaspoon salt

1 teaspoon chives, chopped

Method

1. Mix up all ingredients in the instant pot.

2. Set the "Manual" mode and turn on the timer on 8 minutes (High pressure).

3. When the time is finished, make a quick pressure release.

4. Use the hand blender to make the cream soup smooth.

Nutritional info per serve: calories 322, fat 31.1, fiber 5.4, carbs 12.3, protein 4.8

Pancetta Chowder

Prep time: 5 minutes | **Cook time:** 8 minutes | **Yield:** 3 servings

Ingredients

1 cup of coconut milk

4 oz pancetta, chopped, fried

1 oz celery stalk, chopped

¼ teaspoon salt

1 teaspoon ground paprika

Method

1. Pour the coconut milk in the instant pot bowl.

2. Add celery stalk in the instant pot bowl too.

3. After this, add salt and paprika.

4. Lock the instant pot lid and seal it.

5. Press the "Manual" mode (High pressure) and set the timer for 3 minutes.

6. Then make naturally pressure release for 5 minutes.

7. Top the cooked chowder with fried pancetta.

Nutritional info per serve: calories 392, fat 35, fiber 2.2, carbs 5.6, protein 16

BEEF AND LAMB

Classic Taco Meat

Prep time: 7 minutes | **Cook time:** 15 minutes | **Yield:** 4 servings

Ingredients

1 oz scallions, chopped

1 ½ cup ground beef

1 teaspoon taco seasonings

1 tablespoon coconut oil

Method

1.   Melt the coconut oil on saute mode.

2.   When the oil is hot, add ground beef and saute it for 5 minutes. Stir the meat occasionally.

3.   Then sprinkle the meat with taco seasonings and mix up well.

4.   Cook the taco meat for 5 minutes more.

5.   Add scallions and stir the mixture well. Cook it on saute mode for 5 minutes.

Nutritional info per serve: calories 131, fat 9.5, fiber 0.2, carbs 1, protein 9.9

Ropa Vieja

Prep time: 10 minutes | **Cook time:** 30 minutes | **Yield:** 6 servings

Ingredients

1-pound beef chuck roast, chopped

1 tablespoon coconut oil

1 teaspoon garlic, diced

1 teaspoon ground coriander

1 teaspoon chili powder

1 teaspoon ground paprika

1 cup of water

1 bell pepper, sliced

Method

1.   Pour water in the instant pot.

2.   Add beef. Close and seal the lid.

3.   Cook the meat on manual mode (high pressure) for 20 minutes.

4.   Make a quick pressure release and transfer the meat in the bowl. Clean the instant pot.

5.   Shred the meat well and return back in the instant pot.

6.   Add coconut oil, garlic, ground coriander, chili powder, and ground paprika.

7.   Add sliced bell pepper and mix up the ingredients.

8.   Saute the meal for 10 minutes. Stir it with the help of the spatula from time to time.

Nutritional info per serve: calories 303, fat 23.5, fiber 0.6, carbs 2.1, protein 20.1

Beef Bone Broth

Prep time: 20 minutes | **Cook time:** 50 minutes | **Yield:** 4 servings

Ingredients

1-pound T-bone beef steak, chopped

1 teaspoon salt

1 teaspoon peppercorns

1 bay leaf

3 cups of water

Method

1. Put all ingredients in the instant pot. Close and seal the lid.

2. Then set manual mode (high pressure) and cook the mixture for 50 minutes.

3. Allow the natural pressure release for 15 minutes and open the lid.

4. Strain the cooked mixture and shred the meat.

5. The beef broth should be served with shredded beef.

Nutritional info per serve: calories 303, fat 23.1, fiber 0.2, carbs 0.5, protein 22.1

Ground Beef Okra

Prep time: 10 minutes | **Cook time:** 20 minutes | **Yield:** 4 servings

Ingredients

1 cup okra, sliced

7 oz ground beef

1 teaspoon salt

1 cup of water

1 tablespoon avocado oil

1 teaspoon ground black pepper

Method

1. Heat up avocado oil in the instant pot and add ground beef.

2. Sprinkle it with salt and ground black pepper and saute for 10 minutes.

3. After this, add sliced okra and stir the mixture well.

4. Cook the meal on saute mode for 10 minutes.

Nutritional info per serve: calories 108, fat 3.6, fiber 1.1, carbs 2.4, protein 15.6

Big Mac Salad

Prep time: 10 minutes | **Cook time:** 9 minutes | **Yield:** 2 servings

Ingredients

1 cup lettuce, chopped

2 oz dill pickles, sliced

5 oz ground beef

1 oz scallions, chopped

¼ cup Monterey Jack cheese, shredded

1 tablespoon sesame oil

1 tablespoon heavy cream

1 teaspoon ground black pepper

Method

1. In the mixing bowl, mix up ground beef and ground black pepper. Make the mini burgers.

2. Pour sesame oil in the instant pot and saute it for 3 minutes.

3. Place the mini hamburgers in the hot oil and cook them for 3 minutes from each side.

4. Meanwhile, in the big salad bowl mix up chopped lettuce, dill pickles, scallions, shredded cheese, and heavy cream. Shake the salad mixture well.

5. Top the salad with cooked mini burgers.

Nutritional info per serve: calories 284, fat 18.5, fiber 1.2, carbs 3.5, protein 25.7

Sirloin Roast

Prep time: 10 minutes | **Cook time:** 55 minutes | **Yield:** 4 servings

Ingredients

1 teaspoon pot roast seasonings

16 oz beef sirloin, roughly chopped

1 cup of water

1 tablespoon sesame oil

Method

1. Rub the beef sirloin with pot roast seasonings and sesame oil and wrap in the foil.

2. After this, pour water and insert the steamer rack in the instant pot.

3. Place the wrapped meat on the rack. Close and seal the lid.

4. Cook the sirloin on manual mode (high pressure) for 55 minutes.

5. Then make a quick pressure release and open the lid.

6. Slice the sirloin roast into the servings.

Nutritional info per serve: calories 245, fat 10.5, fiber 0, carbs 0.5, protein 34.7

Mexican Pot Roast

Prep time: 10 minutes | **Cook time:** 55 minutes | **Yield:** 4 servings

Ingredients

1 tablespoon Mexican style seasonings

12 oz beef chuck pot roast, sliced

1 tablespoon butter

1 garlic clove, diced

1 cup of water

Method

1. Toss the butter in the instant pot.

2. Add garlic and saute the ingredients for 3 minutes.

3. Meanwhile, rub the beef chuck roast with Mexican style seasonings.

4. Place the meat in the garlic butter and saute for 6 minutes from each side.

5. Then add water. Close and seal the lid.

6. Cook the Mexican pot roast for 40 minutes on manual mode (high pressure). Make a quick pressure release.

Nutritional info per serve: calories 309, fat 23.1, fiber 0, carbs 0.3, protein 23.4

Beef Tips

Prep time: 10 minutes | **Cook time:** 55 minutes | **Yield:** 4 servings

Ingredients

1-pound chopped beef

1 cup beef broth

1 tablespoon almond flour

1 teaspoon ground black pepper

½ teaspoon cayenne pepper

1 teaspoon salt

½ cup heavy cream

Method

1. Pour beef broth and heavy cream in the instant pot.

2. Add ground black pepper, cayenne pepper, and salt.

3. Then add chopped beef. Close and seal the lid.

4. Cook the beef tips on manual mode (high pressure) for 40 minutes.

5. When the cooking time is finished, allow the natural pressure release for 10 minutes and then remove the meat from the instant pot

6. Add almond flour in the beef liquid and stir until smooth. Cook it on saute mode for 10 minutes.

7. Serve the beef tips with thick beef gravy.

Nutritional info per serve: calories 314, fat 16.5, fiber 1, carbs 2.6, protein 37.5

Low Carb Barbacoa

Prep time: 10 minutes | **Cook time:** 60 minutes | **Yield:** 2 servings

Ingredients

1 tablespoon chipotle peppers in Adobo sauce

1 cup chicken broth

1 tablespoon lemon juice

1 teaspoon sesame oil

8 oz beef sirloin, chopped

Method

1. Put all ingredients in the instant pot. Close and seal the lid.

2. Cook the meal on manual mode (high pressure) for 60 minutes.

3. Then allow the natural pressure release and open the lid.

4. You can shred the meat with the help of the fork if desired.

Nutritional info per serve: calories 255, fat 10.3, fiber 0.5, carbs 0.9, protein 37.1

Bo Kho

Prep time: 20 minutes | **Cook time:** 38 minutes | **Yield:** 4 servings

Ingredients

10 oz beef stew meat, chopped

1 teaspoon curry powder

1 teaspoon tomato paste

½ teaspoon ginger paste

½ cup of coconut milk

1 cup of water

1 cup turnip, chopped

Method

1. Sprinkle the beef stew meat cubes with curry powder.

2. Then place the meat in the instant pot and cook it on saute mode for 3 minutes.

3. Stir it well and add tomato paste, ginger paste, coconut milk, water, and turnip.

4. Close and seal the lid.

5. Cook Bo Kho for 35 minutes on manual mode (high pressure). Then allow the natural pressure release for 7 minutes.

Nutritional info per serve: calories 213, fat 11.7, fiber 1.5, carbs 4.5, protein 22.6

Cauli Beef Burger

Prep time: 15 minutes | **Cook time:** 15 minutes | **Yield:** 2 servings

Ingredients

½ cup cauliflower, shredded

5 oz ground beef

1 teaspoon garlic salt

¼ teaspoon ground cumin

1 tablespoon scallions, diced

1 egg, beaten

1 tablespoon coconut oil

¼ cup hot water

Method

1. In the mixing bowl, mix up shredded cauliflower, ground beef, garlic salt, ground cumin, and diced scallions.

2. When the meat mixture is homogenous, add egg and stir it well.

3. Make the burgers from the cauli-meat mixture.

4. After this, heat up the coconut oil on saute mode.

5. Place the burgers in the hot oil in one layer and cook them for 5 minutes from each side.

6. Then add water and close the lid. Cook the meal on saute mode for 5 minutes more.

Nutritional info per serve: calories 235, fat 13.5, fiber 0.9, carbs 2.9, protein 25.1

Thick Beef Gravy

Prep time: 10 minutes | **Cook time:** 35 minutes | **Yield:** 2 servings

Ingredients

3 oz Brussel sprouts

1 cup beef broth

4 oz pork loin, chopped

½ daikon, chopped

1 teaspoon salt

1 tablespoon coconut flour

1 tablespoon butter

1 cup of water

Method

1. Put all ingredients in the instant pot.

2. Close and seal the lid and cook the mixture on manual mode (high pressure) for 30 minutes.

3. Then make a quick pressure release and open the lid.

4. Blend the mixture with the help of the immersion blender and saute it for 5 minutes.

Nutritional info per serve: calories 246, fat 15.1, fiber 3.3, carbs 7.1, protein 20.4

Beef Bake with Chives

Prep time: 15 minutes | **Cook time:** 25 minutes | **Yield:** 3 servings

Ingredients

12 oz ground beef

1 tablespoon chives, chopped

1 tablespoon fresh parsley, chopped

½ teaspoon salt

1 egg, beaten

1 cup Mozzarella, shredded

1 cup of water

Method

1. In the mixing bowl, mix up ground beef, chives, parsley, salt, and egg.

2. When the mixture is homogenous, transfer it in the big baking ramekin.

3. Top the surface of the meat with Mozzarella and wrap in the foil.

4. Pour water and insert the steamer rack in the instant pot.

5. Place the ramekin with the beef bake on the rack. Close and seal the lid.

6. Cook the meal on manual mode (high pressure) for 25 minutes.

7. Then allow the natural pressure release for 10 minutes.

Nutritional info per serve: calories 259, fat 10.2, fiber 0.1, carbs 0.6, protein 39

Chili Beef Sticks

Prep time: 15 minutes | **Cook time:** 10 minutes | **Yield:** 2 servings

Ingredients

¼ teaspoon ground coriander

½ teaspoon salt

½ teaspoon chili powder

6 oz ground beef

1 tablespoon avocado oil

Method

1.   In the mixing bowl, mix up ground coriander, salt, chili powder, and ground beef.

2.   Then brush the instant pot bowl with avocado oil and heat up on saute mode.

3.   Meanwhile, make the small beef sticks.

4.   Put them in the instant pot and cook on saute mode for 4 minutes from each side or until the beef sticks are light crunchy.

5.   Dry the cooked meat sticks with the help of the paper towel.

Nutritional info per serve: calories 169, fat 6.3, fiber 0.5, carbs 0.8, protein 26

Beef Stuffed Kale

Prep time: 15 minutes | **Cook time:** 30 minutes | **Yield:** 4 servings

Ingredients

4 kale leaves

8 oz ground beef

1 teaspoon chives

¼ teaspoon cayenne pepper

½ cup chicken broth

¼ cup heavy cream

1 tablespoon cream cheese

Method

1.   In the mixing bowl, mix up ground beef, chives, and cayenne pepper.

2.   Then fill and roll the kale leaves with ground beef mixture.

3.   Place the kale rolls in the instant pot.

4.   Add heavy cream, cream cheese, and chicken broth. Close and seal the lid.

5.   Cook the meal on manual mode (high pressure) for 30 minutes + make a quick pressure release.

Nutritional info per serve: calories 153, fat 7.4, fiber 0.3, carbs 2.2, protein 18.7

Oregano Beef Sirloin

Prep time: 10 minutes | **Cook time:** 15 minutes | **Yield:** 2 servings

Ingredients

1 cup of water

¼ cup of coconut milk

14 oz beef sirloin, chopped

1 teaspoon dried oregano

Method

1.   Put all ingredients in the instant pot. Close and seal the lid.

2.   Cook the meal on "Manual" mode (High pressure) for 15 minutes.

3.   Use the quick pressure release.

Nutritional info per serve: calories 440, fat 19.6, fiber 1, carbs 2.1, protein 61

Beef Meatloaf with Chives

Prep time: 10 minutes | **Cook time:** 10 minutes | **Yield:** 4 servings

Ingredients

10 oz ground beef

1 egg, beaten

½ teaspoon salt

1 teaspoon smoked paprika

3 tablespoons water

1 tablespoon chives, chopped

1 cup water, for cooking

Method

1.   In the mixing bowl, mix up ground beef, egg, salt, smoked paprika, 3 tablespoons of water, and chives.

2.   Take the loaf pan and place the meat mixture there.

3.   Flatten it well to make the shape of the meatloaf.

4.   Pour 1 cup of water in the instant pot.

5.   Insert the trivet in the instant pot and place the meatloaf pan on it.

6.   Cook the meal on High pressure (QPR) for 10 minutes.

Nutritional info per serve: calories 149, fat 5.6, fiber 0.2, carbs 0.4, protein 23

Almond Butter Beef

Prep time: 10 minutes | **Cook time:** 60 minutes | **Yield:** 3 servings

Ingredients

10 oz beef chuck roast, chopped

½ cup almond butter

½ teaspoon cayenne pepper

½ teaspoon salt

1 teaspoon dried basil

1 cup of water

Method

1.   Place the almond butter in the instant pot and start to preheat it on the "Saute" mode.

2.   Meanwhile, mix up together the cayenne pepper, salt, and dried basil.

3.   Sprinkle the beef with the spices and transfer the meat in the melted almond butter.

4.   Close the instant pot lid and lock it.

5.   Set the "Manual" mode and put a timer on 60 minutes (Low Pressure).

Nutritional info per serve: calories 360, fat 27.8, fiber 0.4, carbs 0.7, protein 25.3

Creamy Beef Strips

Prep time: 6 minutes | **Cook time:** 20 minutes | **Yield:** 3 servings

Ingredients

½ teaspoon salt

14 oz beef brisket, cut into the strips

½ cup of water

½ cup heavy cream

½ teaspoon ground black pepper

1 tablespoon avocado oil

Method

1.   Preheat the instant pot on the "Saute" mode.

2.   When it is displayed "hot" – pour avocado oil inside and heat it up.

3.   Add the meat.

4. Sprinkle the meat with the ground black pepper and salt.

5. Saute it for 5 minutes. Stir it once per cooking time.

6. Add water and heavy cream.

7. Seal the lid and set the "manual" mode.

8. Put the timer on 15 minutes (High Pressure).

9. Make a quick pressure release.

Nutritional info per serve: calories 322, fat 16.2, fiber 0.3, carbs 1.1, protein 40.6

Cumin Chili

Prep time: 5 minutes | **Cook time:** 15 minutes | **Yield:** 2 servings

Ingredients

13 oz ground beef

1 tablespoon cumin seeds

½ teaspoon salt

1 tablespoon tomato paste

½ teaspoon garlic powder

1 cup of water

Method

1. Preheat the instant pot bowl on the "Saute" mode until it is displayed "Hot".

2. Then place the ground beef there.

3. Sprinkle it with the cumin seeds, garlic powder, and salt.

4. Stir gently and saute for 4 minutes.

5. After this, add tomato paste.

6. Add water and close the lid.

7. Saute the chili for 10 minutes.

8. When the chili is cooked – transfer it directly into the serving bowls.

Nutritional info per serve: calories 362, fat 12.2, fiber 0.7, carbs 3.4, protein 56.9

Cardamom Stew Meat

Prep time: 10 minutes | **Cook time:** 50 minutes | **Yield:** 2 servings

Ingredients

9 oz beef stew meat, chopped

1 teaspoon ground cardamom

½ teaspoon salt

1 cup broccoli, chopped

1 cup of water

Method

1. Preheat the instant pot on the "Saute" mode.

2. When the title "Hot" is displayed – add chopped beef stew meat and cook it for 4 minutes (for 2 minutes from each side).

3. Then add the ground cardamom, salt, and broccoli.

4. Add water and close the instant pot lid.

5. Saute the stew for 45 minutes – to get the tender taste.

6. Enjoy!

Nutritional info per serve: calories 256, fat 8.2, fiber 1.5, carbs 3.7, protein 40.1

Easy Taco Stuffing

Prep time: 5 minutes | **Cook time:** 11 minutes | **Yield:** 2 servings

Ingredients

1 teaspoon taco seasoning

9 oz ground beef

¼ cup beef broth

1 teaspoon tomato paste

Method

1. Place the ground beef and taco seasonings in the instant pot bowl.

2. Start to saute the meat. Cook it for 5 minutes.

3. After this, add beef broth and tomato paste.

4. Stir it well.

5. Set the "Manual" mode (High pressure) and cook the meat for 6 minutes more.

6. After this, use the quick pressure release method.

Nutritional info per serve: calories 249, fat 8.1, fiber 0.1, carbs 1.6, protein 39.4

Blackberry Beef

Prep time: 15 minutes | **Cook time:** 30 minutes | **Yield:** 2 servings

Ingredients

15 oz beef loin, chopped

1 tablespoon blackberries

1 cup of water

½ teaspoon ground cinnamon

1/3 teaspoon ground black pepper

½ teaspoon salt

1 tablespoon butter

Method

1. Pour water in the instant pot bowl.

2. Add chopped beef loin, blackberries, ground cinnamon, salt, and ground black pepper. Add butter.

3. Close the instant pot lid and set the "Meat" mode.

4. Cook the meat for 30 minutes. Then remove the meat from the instant pot. Blend the remaining blackberry mixture.

5. Pour it over the meat.

Nutritional info per serve: calories 372, fat 21, fiber 0.6, carbs 3.7, protein 39.4

Moroccan Anise Stew

Prep time: 5 minutes | **Cook time:** 50 minutes | **Yield:** 3 servings

Ingredients

½ cup of coconut milk

1 teaspoon butter

½ teaspoon dried rosemary

¼ teaspoon salt

½ teaspoon ground coriander

13 oz lamb shoulder, chopped

1 teaspoon ground anise

¾ cup of water

Method

1. Slice the mushrooms and place them in the instant pot bowl.

2. Add all remaining ingredients. Close and seal the lid.

3. Set "Manual" mode for 45 minutes.

4. When the time is over – make natural pressure release for 10 minutes.

Nutritional info per serve: calories 332, fat 19.8, fiber 1, carbs 2.4, protein 35.4

Chinese Beef

Prep time: 8 minutes | **Cook time:** 13 minutes | **Yield:** 2 servings

Ingredients

14 oz beef flank steak, sliced

1 tablespoon almond flour

½ teaspoon minced ginger

1 oz scallions, sliced

1 tablespoon coconut oil

¾ cup of water

Method

1.   Toss the beef strips in the almond flour and shake well.

2.   Toss the coconut oil in the instant pot bowl and set the "saute" mode.

3.   When the coconut oil is melted – add the beef flank steak slices and cook them for 3 minutes. Stir them from time to time.

4.   Add minced ginger.

5.   Pour the water over the meat and lock the instant pot lid.

6.   Press the "Manual" mode (High pressure) and set the timer for 10 minutes.

7.   Make a quick pressure release.

8.   Top the cooked beef with sliced scallions.

Nutritional info per serve: calories 513, fat 26.2, fiber 1.9, carbs 4.4, protein 63.5

Succulent Beef Ribs

Prep time: 10 minutes | **Cook time:** 40 minutes | **Yield:** 2 servings

Ingredients

10 oz beef ribs

¾ cup of water

2 tablespoons coconut oil

1 teaspoon dried marjoram

½ teaspoon salt

½ cup chicken broth

Method

1.   Rub the beef ribs with the dried marjoram and salt.

2.   Place the beef ribs in the instant pot bowl.

3.   Add chicken broth and water.

4.   Then add coconut oil.

5.   Close the lid and set the "Meat" mode. Cook the ribs for 40 minutes.

Nutritional info per serve: calories 391, fat 22.8, fiber 0.1, carbs 0.4, protein 44.3

Beef Cakes Stew

Prep time: 15 minutes | **Cook time:** 10 minutes | **Yield:** 2 servings

Ingredients

10 oz ground beef

½ teaspoon white pepper

½ teaspoon ground paprika

½ cup of water

½ teaspoon turmeric

1 zucchini, chopped

1 teaspoon butter

1 tablespoon scallions, chopped

Method

1.   Mix up together the ground beef, white pepper, ground paprika, turmeric and make the small meat cakes.

2.   Place the meat cakes in the instant pot bowl.

3.   Add butter and cook them on saute mode for 2 minutes from each side.

4.   Then add chopped scallions, water, and zucchini.

5.   Lock the instant pot lid and set "Manual" mode (High Pressure) for 10 minutes. Then make a quick release.

6.   Transfer the cooked stew in the bowls.

Nutritional info per serve: calories 302, fat 11.1, fiber 1.6, carbs 4.5, protein 44.4

BBQ Pulled Beef

Prep time: 10 minutes | **Cook time:** 40 minutes | **Yield:** 2 servings

Ingredients

9 oz beef loin

1 cup of water

½ cup BBQ sauce (keto-friendly)

Method

1.   Put all ingredients in the instant pot.

2.   Close and seal the lid.

3.   Cook the beef on manual (high pressure) for 40 minutes.

4.   Then make a quick pressure release and shred the beef with the help of the forks.

Nutritional info per serve: calories 267, fat 13.2, fiber 1, carbs 3, protein 35.1

Vegetable Lasagna with Meat

Prep time: 15 minutes | **Cook time:** 20 minutes | **Yield:** 2 servings

Ingredients

1 large zucchini, grated

8 oz ground beef

1 tablespoon coconut milk

1 oz provolone cheese, shredded

½ tomato, sliced

1 teaspoon butter, softened

1 cup water, for cooking

Method

1.   Grease the lasagna mold with butter.

2.   Put ½ part of zucchini in the mold and flatten it.

3.   Then add ground beef, coconut milk, and sliced tomato.

4.   Then top the ingredients with remaining zucchini and flatten well.

5.   Pour water and insert the lasagna mold in the into the instant pot.

6.   Close and seal the lid.

7.   Cook the meal on manual (high pressure) for 20 minutes. Then make a quick pressure release.

Nutritional info per serve: calories 323, fat 14.9, fiber 2.1, carbs 6.7, protein 40.3

PORK

Pork Chops Marsala

Prep time: 20 minutes | **Cook time:** 25 minutes | **Yield:** 2 servings

Ingredients

2 pork chops

½ cup cremini mushrooms, sliced

¼ cup apple cider vinegar

1 tablespoon coconut oil

1 teaspoon dried thyme

½ cup heavy cream

¼ cup chicken broth

Method

1. Put all ingredients in the instant pot.
2. Close and seal the lid.
3. Cook the pork on manual mode (high pressure) for 25 minutes.
4. Allow the natural pressure release for 15 minutes and open the lid.
5. Stir the pork chop marsala well before serving.

Nutritional info per serve: calories 435, fat 38, fiber 0.3, carbs 2.3, protein 19.7

Pork and Sauerkraut Mix

Prep time: 10 minutes | **Cook time:** 15 minutes | **Yield:** 4 servings

Ingredients

4 pork chops, chopped

½ teaspoon cayenne pepper

½ teaspoon ground coriander

1 tablespoon coconut oil

1 tablespoon avocado oil

1 cup sauerkraut

Method

1. Melt the coconut oil on saute mode.
2. Add cayenne pepper, ground coriander, and chopped pork chops.
3. Cook the meat on saute mode for 7 minutes from each side.
4. Then transfer the cooked meat in the bowl, add sauerkraut and mix up well.

Nutritional info per serve: calories 297, fat 23.8, fiber 1.2, carbs 1.9, protein 18.4

Ground Salisbury Steak

Prep time: 10 minutes | **Cook time:** 25 minutes | **Yield:** 4 servings

Ingredients

1 cup ground pork

1 teaspoon chili flakes

1 teaspoon dried cilantro

1 cup chicken broth

1 teaspoon olive oil

1 tablespoon mustard

1 cup white mushrooms, chopped

Method

1. Put olive oil and mushrooms in the instant pot.
2. Add dried cilantro, and chili flakes and cook the ingredients for 10 minutes on saute mode.
3. Then add mustard and ground pork.

4.   Add chicken broth. Close and seal the lid.

5.   Cook the meat on manual mode (high pressure) for 15 minutes.

6.   Make a quick pressure release.

Nutritional info per serve: calories 94, fat 6.4, fiber 0.6, carbs 1.8, protein 7.5

Adobo Pork

Prep time: 10 minutes | **Cook time:** 30 minutes | **Yield:** 6 servings

Ingredients

1-pound pork belly, chopped

1 bay leaf

1 teaspoon salt

2 tablespoons apple cider vinegar

1 teaspoon cayenne pepper

1 garlic clove, peeled

2 cups of water

Method

1.   Put all ingredients in the instant pot.

2.   Close and seal the lid.

3.   Cook Adobo pork for 30 minutes on manual mode (high pressure).

4.   When the cooking time is finished, make a quick pressure release and transfer the pork belly in the bowls.

5.   Add 1 ladle of the pork gravy.

Nutritional info per serve: calories 352, fat 20.4, fiber 0.1, carbs 0.5, protein 35

Kalua Pork

Prep time: 10 minutes | **Cook time:** 10 hours | **Yield:** 4 servings

Ingredients

1-pound pork butt

1 teaspoon salt

½ teaspoon liquid smoke

1 cucumber, chopped

1 tomato, chopped

½ bell pepper, chopped

Method

1.   Rub the meat with salt and liquid smoke and put it in the instant pot.

2.   Close the lid and cook it on "low" for 10 hours.

3.   Meanwhile, mix up together cucumber, tomato, and bell pepper.

4.   Shred the cooked meat and put it in the serving bowls.

5.   Top the meat with vegetable mixture.

Nutritional info per serve: calories 238, fat 7.7, fiber 0.8, carbs 4.5, protein 36.1

Garlic Italian Sausages

Prep time: 15 minutes | **Cook time:** 20 minutes | **Yield:** 4 servings

Ingredients

1 teaspoon garlic powder

1 cup of water

1 teaspoon butter

12 oz Italian sausages, chopped

½ teaspoon Italian seasonings

Method

1.   Sprinkle the chopped Italian sausages with Italian seasonings and garlic powder and place in the instant pot.

2. Add butter and cook the sausages on saute mode for 10 minutes. Stir them from time to time with the help of the spatula.

3. Then add water and close the lid.

4. Cook the sausages on manual mode (high pressure) for 10 minutes.

5. Allow the natural pressure release for 10 minutes more.

Nutritional info per serve: calories 307, fat 27.8, fiber 0.1, carbs 1.1, protein 12.3

Pork Loin in Vegetable Gravy

Prep time: 10 minutes | **Cook time:** 50 minutes | **Yield:** 4 servings

Ingredients

1-pound pork loin

½ cup cauliflower, chopped

1 daikon, chopped

2 oz celery stalk, chopped

1 teaspoon salt

1 teaspoon peppercorns

2 cups of water

1 tablespoon almond flour

Method

1. Put the pork loin in the instant pot.

2. Add cauliflower, chopped daikon, celery stalk, salt, peppercorns, and water.

3. Close and seal the lid and cook the meat on manual mode (high pressure) for 40 minutes.

4. Then make a quick pressure release and open the lid.

5. Transfer the meat on the plate.

6. Add the almond flour in the remaining mixture in the instant pot and with the help of the immersion blender, blend the mixture until smooth.

7. Saute the gravy for 10 minutes.

8. Pour the cooked gravy over the meat.

Nutritional info per serve: calories 324, fat 19.3, fiber 1.7, carbs 3.4, protein 33.1

Light Posole

Prep time: 10 minutes | **Cook time:** 35 minutes | **Yield:** 4 servings

Ingredients

1 teaspoon Ancho chili powder

½ teaspoon ground coriander

½ teaspoon of cocoa powder

1-pound pork shoulder, boneless, chopped

2 cups beef broth

Method

1. Put ground coriander, beef broth, and cocoa powder in the instant pot.

2. Stir the mixture until the beef broth will turn color into chocolate.

3. Add Ancho chili powder, and pork shoulder.

4. Close the lid.

5. Cook the meal on meat/stew mode for 35 minutes.

Nutritional info per serve: calories 351, fat 25, fiber 0.1, carbs 0.6, protein 28.9

Sweet Ham

Prep time: 10 minutes | **Cook time:** 7 minutes | **Yield:** 6 servings

Ingredients

1-pound ham

½ cup butter

3 tablespoons Erythritol

½ teaspoon cumin seeds

1 cup water, for cooking

Method

1.   Pour water in the instant pot and insert the steamer rack.

2.   After this, in the mixing bowl, mix up Erythritol, butter, and cumin seeds.

3.   Brush the ham with the sweet mixture well and transfer it in the instant pot.

4.   Add the remaining sweet mixture. Close and seal the lid.

5.   Cook the ham on manual mode (high pressure) for 7 minutes.

6.   Make a quick pressure release and slice the ham.

Nutritional info per serve: calories 260, fat 21.9, fiber 1, carbs 3, protein 12.7

Pork Florentine

Prep time: 20 minutes | **Cook time:** 45 minutes | **Yield:** 6 servings

Ingredients

12 oz pork roast, roll cut

1 cup spinach

3 oz Monterey Jack cheese, shredded

1 tablespoon olive oil

½ teaspoon ground black pepper

1 cup water, for cooking

Method

1.   Beet the pork roast with the help of the kitchen hammer.

2.   After this, put the spinach in the blender and add olive oil, and ground black pepper. Blend the mixture until smooth.

3.   Then transfer the mixture over the pork roast, spread it well and top with shredded cheese.

4.   Roll the meat and wrap in the foil.

5.   Pour water and insert the steamer rack in the instant pot.

6.   Put the wrapped pork on the steamer rack. Close and seal the lid.

7.   Cook the meal on manual mode (high pressure) for 45 minutes.

8.   Allow the natural pressure release for 15 minutes.

Nutritional info per serve: calories 298, fat 20.6, fiber 0.2, carbs 0.6, protein 26.7

Tangy Pork

Prep time: 10 minutes | **Cook time:** 40 minutes | **Yield:** 3 servings

Ingredients

8 oz pork loin

1 teaspoon keto ketchup

1 cup of water

3 tablespoons coconut aminos

½ teaspoon garlic powder

1 tablespoon Splenda

½ teaspoon cayenne pepper

Method

1. Cut the pork loin on 3 servings and put in the instant pot.

2. Add keto ketchup, water, coconut aminos, garlic powder, Splenda, and cayenne pepper.

3. Stir the mixture gently and close the lid.

4. Cook the tangy pork on meat/stew mode for 40 minutes.

Nutritional info per serve: calories 222, fat 10.6, fiber 0.1, carbs 7.9, protein 20.8

Filipino Pork

Prep time: 10 minutes | **Cook time:** 40 minutes | **Yield:** 4 servings

Ingredients

1-pound pork loin, chopped

½ cup apple cider vinegar

1 cup chicken broth

1 chili pepper, chopped

1 tablespoon coconut oil

1 teaspoon salt

Method

1. Melt the coconut oil on saute mode.

2. When it is hot, and chili pepper and cook it for 2 minutes. Stir it.

3. Add chopped pork loin and salt. Cook the ingredients for 5 minutes.

4. After this, add apple cider vinegar and chicken broth.

5. Close and seal the lid and cook the Filipino pork for 30 minutes on High pressure (manual mode). Then make a quick pressure release.

Nutritional info per serve: calories 320, fat 19.5, fiber 0, carbs 0.6, protein 32.2

Cuban Pork

Prep time: 20 minutes | **Cook time:** 35 minutes | **Yield:** 3 servings

Ingredients

9 oz pork shoulder, boneless, chopped

1 tablespoon avocado oil

1 teaspoon ground cumin

½ teaspoon ground black pepper

¼ cup apple cider vinegar

1 cup of water

Method

1. In the mixing bowl, mix up avocado oil, ground cumin, ground black pepper, and apple cider vinegar.

2. Mix up pork shoulder and spice mixture together and transfer on the foil. Wrap the meat mixture.

3. Pour water and insert the steamer rack in the instant pot.

4. Put the wrapped pork shoulder on the rack. Close and seal the lid.

5. Cook the Cuban pork for 35 minutes.

6. Then allow the natural pressure release for 10 minutes.

Nutritional info per serve: calories 262, fat 19, fiber 0.4, carbs 1, protein 20

Cheesesteak Meatloaf

Prep time: 15 minutes | **Cook time:** 40 minutes | **Yield:** 4 servings

Ingredients

1 cup ground pork

½ cup Cheddar cheese, shredded

2 tablespoons almond flour

1 tablespoon chives, chopped

1 teaspoon pork seasonings

1 egg, beaten

1 cup water, for cooking

Method

1.   Put the ground pork in the bowl.

2.   Add almond flour, chives, pork seasonings, and egg.

3.   Mix up the mixture until smooth.

4.   After this, place ½ part of the mixture in the loaf mold, flatten it well and top with ½ part of all Cheddar cheese.

5.   Then add remaining ground pork mixture and cheese.

6.   Pour water and insert the steamer rack in the instant pot.

7.   Place the meatloaf on the rack. Close and seal the lid.

8.   Cook the meal on manual mode (high pressure) for 40 minutes. Make a quick pressure release.

Nutritional info per serve: calories 326, fat 23.7, fiber 0.4, carbs 1, protein 25.8

Eggplant Lasagna

Prep time: 20 minutes | **Cook time:** 30 minutes | **Yield:** 6 servings

Ingredients

10 oz ground pork

1 cup Mozzarella, shredded

1 tablespoon tomato paste

2 eggplants, sliced

1 teaspoon salt

1 teaspoon butter, softened

1 cup chicken stock

Method

1.   Sprinkle the eggplants with salt and leave for 10 minutes.

2.   Then make the eggplants dry with the help of the pepper towel.

3.   In the mixing bowl, mix up ground pork, butter, and tomato paste.

4.   Make the layer of the sliced eggplants in the instant pot and top it with the thin layer of ground pork mixture.

5.   Then top the ground pork with Mozzarella and repeat all the steps again till you use all ingredients.

6.   Add chicken stock.

7.   Close and seal the lid.

8.   Cook the lasagna on manual mode for 30 minutes.

9.   Then allow the natural pressure release for 10 minutes and open the lid.

10.   Cool the meal for 10 minutes.

Nutritional info per serve: calories 136, fat 3.6, fiber 6.6, carbs 11.5, protein 15.7

Pork Dumpling Meatballs

Prep time: 10 minutes | **Cook time:** 19 minutes | **Yield:** 2 servings

Ingredients

6 oz ground pork

1 teaspoon minced garlic

½ teaspoon chives, chopped

1 teaspoon coconut aminos

½ teaspoon cayenne pepper

1 tablespoon coconut oil

1 teaspoon ginger paste

½ cup chicken broth

Method

1. In the bowl, mix up ground pork, minced garlic, chives, coconut aminos, cayenne pepper, and ginger paste.

2. Make the small balls (dumplings) from the meat mixture.

3. After this, melt the coconut oil and put the meatballs inside.

4. Roast them on saute mode for 1 minute from each side.

5. Then add chicken broth and close the lid.

6. Saute the meal on saute mode for 15 minutes.

Nutritional info per serve: calories 199, fat 10.3, fiber 0.3, carbs 2.1, protein 23.7

Pork Cubes in Sauce

Prep time: 8 minutes | **Cook time:** 30 minutes | **Yield:** 2 servings

Ingredients

1 teaspoon lemon juice

10 oz pork loin, chopped

½ cup of water

1 oz fennel, chopped

1 teaspoon salt

½ teaspoon peppercorns

Method

1. Sprinkle the chopped pork loin with the lemon juice.

2. Then strew the meat with the salt.

3. Place the meat in the meat mold.

4. Insert the meat mold in the instant pot.

5. Add water, fennel, and peppercorns.

6. Close the lid and lock it.

7. Set the "Meat" mode and put a timer on 30 minutes.

8. Serve the pork cubes with hot gravy.

Nutritional info per serve: calories 349, fat 19.8, fiber 0.6, carbs 1.4, protein 39

Tender Pork Liver

Prep time: 5 minutes | **Cook time:** 7 minutes | **Yield:** 3 servings

Ingredients

14 oz pork liver, chopped

½ cup heavy cream

3 tablespoons scallions, chopped

1 teaspoon salt

1 teaspoon butter

Method

1. Sprinkle the liver with the salt.

2. Toss the butter in the instant pot and melt it on the "Saute" mode.

3. Add heavy cream, scallions, and liver.

4. Stir gently and close the lid.

5. Cook the meal on the "Saute" mode for 12 minutes.

Nutritional info per serve: calories 300, fat 14.5, fiber 0.2, carbs 6, protein 35

Pork Eggplant Halves

Prep time: 15 minutes | **Cook time:** 5 minutes |
Yield: 2 servings

Ingredients

1 eggplant, halved

10 oz ground pork

½ teaspoon minced garlic

½ teaspoon salt

1 tablespoon butter

1 teaspoon tomato paste

Method

1.   Remove ½ of pulp from the eggplants.

2.   Mix up together the minced garlic, salt, tomato paste, and ground pork.

3.   Fill the eggplants with the pork mixture.

4.   Cover the eggplant halves with the butter.

5.   Wrap the eggplants into the foil and transfer them on the steamer rack in the instant pot.

6.   Pour 1 cup of water in the instant pot and close the lid.

7.   Cook the eggplants on High Pressure (Steam mode) for 7 minutes.

8.   Then make the natural pressure release for 5 minutes.

Nutritional info per serve: calories 314, fat 11.2, fiber 8.2, carbs 14.2, protein 39.6

Ginger Meatballs

Prep time: 10 minutes | **Cook time:** 7 minutes |
Yield: 2 servings

Ingredients

1 teaspoon ginger paste

11 oz ground pork

1 teaspoon lemon juice

¼ teaspoon chili flakes

1 tablespoon butter

¼ cup of water

Method

1.   Combine together the ground pork and ginger paste

2.   Add lemon juice, and chili flakes.

3.   Toss the butter in the instant pot bowl and melt it.

4.   Meanwhile, make the small meatballs from the meat mixture.

5.   Place the meatballs in the instant pot and cook for 2 minutes from each side.

6.   After this, add water and lock the lid.

7.   Set the "Manual" mode for 3 minutes (High pressure) + Quick pressure release.

Nutritional info per serve: calories 278, fat 11.3, fiber 0.1, carbs 0.7, protein 41

Smoked Paprika Pulled Pork

Prep time: 7 minutes | **Cook time:** 40 minutes |
Yield: 3 servings

Ingredients

1-pound pork roast, chopped

½ teaspoon ground cumin

1 tablespoon smoked paprika

1 cup beef broth

1 tablespoon coconut oil

1 teaspoon garlic powder

Method

1.   Mix up together garlic powder and ground cumin.

2.   Then combine together the spices and chopped pork roast. Add the smoked paprika.

3.   Place the meat in the instant pot bowl. Add coconut oil and beef broth.

4.   Close the instant pot lid and seal it.

5.   Set the manual mode and put the timer on 30 minutes (High pressure).

6.   Make the natural-release pressure.

7.   Transfer the cooked meat in the bowl and shred it. Serve the meal with meat liquid.

Nutritional info per serve: calories 376, fat 19.6, fiber 1, carbs 2.4, protein 45.3

Bell Peppers with Pork

Prep time: 10minutes | **Cook time:** 15 minutes | **Yield:** 2 servings

Ingredients

8 oz bell peppers, deseeded

5 oz ground beef

¼ teaspoon salt

¾ teaspoon ground black pepper

2 teaspoon cream cheese

½ cup of water

Method

1.   Mix up together the salt, and ground black pepper. Stir it well.

2.   Fill the peppers with the ground beef mixture.

3.   Top every pepper with the cream cheese.

4.   Pour water in the instant pot and add the steam rack.

5.   Place the peppers on the steam rack and close the instant pot lid and seal it.

6.   Set the "Manual" mode and put the timer on 9 minutes. Make NPR (appx. 5 minutes).

Nutritional info per serve: calories 169, fat 5.8, fiber 2.2, carbs 6.1, protein 22.9

Chili Pork Cubes

Prep time: 10 minutes | **Cook time:** 20 minutes | **Yield:** 2 servings

Ingredients

10 oz pork loin

¼ cup of water

1 teaspoon chili paste

½ teaspoon ground black pepper

½ teaspoon salt

Method

1.   Chop the pork loin into the medium pieces.

2.   Sprinkle the meat with the salt and ground black pepper.

3.   add chili paste in the meat.

4.   Mix up the meat mixture with the help of the hands.

5.   Pour water in the instant pot bowl and add meat mixture.

6.   Close the lid and set the "Meat/Stew" mode. Cook the meal for 25 minutes.

7.   Then chill the meat until warm.

Nutritional info per serve: calories 353, fat 20.2, fiber 0.1, carbs 1.3, protein 39

Bacon Sticks

Prep time: 5 minutes | **Cook time:** 5 minutes |
Yield: 4 servings

Ingredients

2 tablespoons almond flour

1 tablespoon water

6 oz bacon, sliced

¾ teaspoon chili pepper

Method

1. Sprinkle the sliced bacon with the almond flour and water. Add chili pepper.

2. Put it in the instant pot in one layer.

3. Cook the meal on the "Saute" program for 6 minutes (cook for 3 minutes per side).

Nutritional info per serve: calories 251, fat 19.4, fiber 0.4, carbs 1.5, protein 16.5

Herbed Butter Pork Chops

Prep time: 5 minutes | **Cook time:** 12 minutes |
Yield: 5 servings

Ingredients

13 oz pork chops

1/2 cup butter, softened

1 tablespoon Italian seasonings

Method

1. Whisk together Italian seasonings and butter.

2. Rub the pork chops with herbed butter and put in the instant pot.

3. Cook the meat on saute mode for 7 minutes from each side.

Nutritional info per serve: calories 407, fat 37.6, fiber 0, carbs 0.3, protein 16.8

Pork Muffins

Prep time: 5 minutes | **Cook time:** 9 minutes |
Yield: 2 servings

Ingredients

2 tablespoons coconut flour

1 egg, beaten

4 oz ground pork, fried

1 teaspoon parsley

¼ teaspoon salt

1 tablespoon coconut cream

Method

1. Whisk the beaten egg with the help of the hand whisker.

2. Stir the coconut flour into the whisked egg and add parsley, salt, and coconut cream. Add cooked ground pork.

3. Mix up the mixture until homogenous.

4. Pour the mixture into the muffin molds.

5. Pour 1 cup of water in the instant pot and place trivet.

6. Transfer the muffin molds on the trivet and close the instant pot lid.

7. Set the "manual" mode and cook the muffins for 4 minutes of +natural pressure release for 5 minutes.

Nutritional info per serve: calories 160, fat 6.7, fiber 3.2, carbs 5.6, protein 18.8

Egg Balls

Prep time: 5 minutes | **Cook time:** 5 minutes | **Yield:** 3 servings

Ingredients

2 eggs

4 oz fried bacon, chopped

1 tablespoon butter

¾ teaspoon salt

1 tablespoon cream cheese

Method

1. Pour 1 cup of water in the instant pot bowl and add eggs. Seal the instant pot lid.

2. Set the "Steam" program and cook the eggs for 5 minutes. Then make a quick release.

3. Meanwhile, melt the butter and mix it up with the salt, bacon, and cream cheese.

4. Chill the cooked eggs, peel them, and chop.

5. Stir together eggs and bacon mixture.

6. Make the egg balls.

Nutritional info per serve: calories 292, fat 23.7, fiber 0, carbs 0.9, protein 18

Pork Quiche

Prep time: 10 minutes | **Cook time:** 6 minutes | **Yield:** 2 servings

Ingredients

3 eggs, beaten

1 tablespoon coconut flour

4 oz Mozzarella, shredded

5 oz ground pork

¼ cup spinach

½ teaspoon salt

1 tablespoon butter

Method

1. Whisk the eggs and coconut flour together.

2. add ground pork in the egg mixture.

3. After this, chop the spinach and add in the egg mixture too.

4. Add butter and mix up the mixture very carefully.

5. Place the mixture into the quiche pan. Sprinkle the mixture with Mozzarella over.

6. Then transfer the pan in the instant pot and close the lid.

7. Set the "Manual" program and cook quiche for 6 minutes + QPR.

8. Cut the quiche into halves.

Nutritional info per serve: calories 422, fat 25.5, fiber 1.6, carbs 5.2, protein 43.5

Spanish Style Pork Shoulder

Prep time: 10 minutes | **Cook time:** 40 minutes | **Yield:** 3 servings

Ingredients

12 oz pork shoulder

½ cup chili Verde

1 tablespoon butter

¼ cup beef broth

¾ teaspoon ground black pepper

½ teaspoon salt

Method

1. Chop the pork shoulder and sprinkle the meat with the ground black pepper and salt.

2. Toss the butter in the instant pot and saute it for 1 minute or until it is melted.

3. After this, add pork shoulder and saute it for 10 minutes.

4. After this, add beef broth and chili Verde.

5. Lock the instant pot lid and seal it.

6. Set the "Bean/Chili" mode and set the timer on 30 minutes (High Pressure).

7. When the time is over – make a natural pressure release.

8. Serve it!

Nutritional info per serve: calories 370, fat 28.2, fiber 0.1, carbs 0.4, protein 26.9

Tender Pork with Salsa Verde

Prep time: 10 minutes | **Cook time:** 40 minutes | **Yield:** 3 servings

Ingredients

12 oz pork shoulder, sliced

½ cup salsa verde

½ cup of water

¾ teaspoon peppercorns

½ teaspoon salt

Method

9. Toss the butter in the instant pot and saute it for 1 minute or until it is melted.

10. After this, add pork shoulder, salt, and peppercorns; saute the ingredients for 10 minutes.

11. After this, add water and salsa verde.

12. Set the "Bean/Chili" mode and set the timer on 30 minutes (High Pressure).

13. When the time is over – make a natural pressure release.

Nutritional info per serve: calories 342, fat 24.4, fiber 0.3, carbs 2.1, protein 27

Shredded Pork Stew

Prep time: 15 minutes | **Cook time:** 35 minutes | **Yield:** 2 servings

Ingredients

16 oz pork chuck roast

½ teaspoon coriander

½ teaspoon salt

1 daikon, chopped

1 cup of water

Method

1. Put all ingredients in the instant pot. Close and seal the lid.

2. After this, set the "Meat" mode and cook the stew for 35 minutes.

3. When the stew is cooked, carefully shred the meat with the help of the fork.

Nutritional info per serve: calories 533, fat 28.8, fiber 0.5, carbs 1, protein 63.6

Fajita Pork Strips

Prep time: 5 minutes | **Cook time:** 45 minutes | **Yield:** 2 servings

Ingredients

11 oz pork shoulder, boneless, sliced

1 teaspoon fajita seasonings

2 tablespoons butter

½ cup of water

Method

1. Sprinkle the meat with fajita seasonings and put in the instant pot.

2. Add butter and cook it on saute mode for 5 minutes.

3. Then stir the pork strips and add water.

4. Seal the instant pot lid and set the "Manual" mode (High pressure).

5. Set timer for 40 minutes.

6. When the time is running out – make the natural pressure release for 10 minutes.

Nutritional info per serve: calories 375, fat 29.9, fiber 0, carbs 0.7, protein 24.3

POULTRY

Spanish Chicken

Prep time: 10 minutes | **Cook time:** 25 minutes | **Yield:** 4 servings

Ingredients

4 chicken thighs, skinless

1 teaspoon tomato paste

2 oz olives, sliced

½ cup chicken broth

1 teaspoon dried oregano

1 tablespoon goat milk butter

Method

1.   Put the goat milk butter in the instant pot and heat it up on saute mode for 2 minutes.

2.   Then add chicken thighs and cook them for 4 minutes from each side.

3.   Add dried oregano, olives, tomato paste, and chicken broth.

4.   Close and seal the lid and cook the Spanish chicken on manual mode (high pressure) for 15 minutes.

5.   Make a quick pressure release.

Nutritional info per serve: calories 328, fat 15.6, fiber 0.7, carbs 1.5, protein 43.1

Hot BBQ Wings

Prep time: 10 minutes | **Cook time:** 30 minutes | **Yield:** 6 servings

Ingredients

1-pound chicken wings

1 teaspoon keto ketchup

½ cup keto BBQ sauce

1 tablespoon avocado oil

¼ cup of water

Method

1.   Heat up avocado oil in the instant pot on saute mode.

2.   Add chicken wings and cook them for 2 minutes from each side.

3.   After this, add all remaining ingredients. Close the lid.

4.   Saute the chicken wings for 25 minutes.

Nutritional info per serve: calories 179, fat 6, fiber 0.2, carbs 7.9, protein 21.9

Mushroom Mini Pizza

Prep time: 10 minutes | **Cook time:** 10 minutes | **Yield:** 4 servings

Ingredients

4 Portobello mushroom caps

2 oz Parmesan, grated

½ tomato, chopped

2 oz ground chicken

1 cup water, for cooking

Method

1.   Pour water and insert the steamer rack in the instant pot.

2.   Then fill the mushroom caps with chopped tomato, ground chicken, and grated Parmesan.

3.   Place the mushroom caps on the rack. Close and seal the lid.

4. Cook the mini pizzas on manual mode (high pressure) for 10 minutes.

5. Then make a quick pressure release and transfer the mini pizzas on the big serving plate.

Nutritional info per serve: calories 81, fat 4.2, fiber 0.5, carbs 2.2, protein 9.4

Vinegar Chicken Fillets

Prep time: 15 minutes | **Cook time:** 25 minutes | **Yield:** 4 servings

Ingredients

1 teaspoon Cajun seasonings

¼ cup apple cider vinegar

1-pound chicken fillet

1 tablespoon sesame oil

¼ cup of water

Method

1. Put all ingredients in the instant pot. Close and seal the lid.

2. Cook the chicken fillets on manual mode (high pressure) for 25 minutes.

3. Allow the natural pressure release for 10 minutes.

Nutritional info per serve: calories 249, fat 11.8, fiber 0, carbs 0.1, protein 32.8

Chicken Shawarma

Prep time: 15 minutes | **Cook time:** 17 minutes | **Yield:** 4 servings

Ingredients

1-pound chicken fillet

½ teaspoon ground coriander

½ teaspoon smoked paprika

½ teaspoon dried thyme

1 tablespoon tahini sauce

1 teaspoon lemon juice

1 teaspoon heavy cream

1 cup water, for cooking

Method

1. Rub the chicken fillet with ground coriander, smoked paprika, thyme, and wrap in the foil.

2. Then pour water and insert the steamer rack in the instant pot.

3. Place the wrapped chicken in the steamer; close and seal the lid.

4. Cook the chicken on manual mode (high pressure) for 17 minutes. Make a quick pressure release.

5. Make the sauce: mix up heavy cream, lemon juice, and tahini paste.

6. Slice the chicken and sprinkle it with sauce.

Nutritional info per serve: calories 234, fat 10, fiber 0.2, carbs 0.8, protein 33.4

Pecan Chicken

Prep time: 10 minutes | **Cook time:** 15 minutes | **Yield:** 2 servings

Ingredients

6 oz chicken fillet, cubed

2 pecans, chopped

1 teaspoon coconut aminos

½ bell pepper, chopped

1 tablespoon coconut oil

¼ cup apple cider vinegar

¼ cup chicken broth

Method

1.   Melt coconut oil on saute mode and add chicken cubes.

2.   Add bell pepper, and pecans.

3.   Saute the ingredients for 10 minutes and add apple cider vinegar, chicken broth, and coconut aminos.

4.   Saute the chicken for 5 minutes more.

Nutritional info per serve: calories 341, fat 23.4, fiber 1.9, carbs 5.1, protein 27

Chicken Slaw Mix

Prep time: 10 minutes | **Cook time:** 15 minutes | **Yield:** 2 servings

Ingredients

½ cup slaw mix

1 tablespoon heavy cream

6 oz chicken, chopped

1 teaspoon ground black pepper

1 tablespoon olive oil

1 teaspoon lemon juice

Method

1.   Put the chicken in the instant pot and sprinkle with lemon juice, ground black pepper, and olive oil.

2.   Stir gently and cook it on saute mode for 15 minutes. Stir it from time to time.

3.   Then cool the cooked chicken gently and mix it up with slaw mix.

4.   Add heavy cream and mix up well.

Nutritional info per serve: calories 236, fat 12.4, fiber 0.3, carbs 5.5, protein 25.1

Low Carb Pot Pie

Prep time: 15 minutes | **Cook time:** 50 minutes | **Yield:** 6 servings

Ingredients

10 oz chicken fillet, chopped

1 teaspoon salt

½ teaspoon ground black pepper

½ cup heavy cream

2 tablespoons scallions, chopped

1 daikon, diced

½ cup Mozzarella, shredded

½ cup coconut flour

2 eggs, beaten

Cooking spray

1 cup water, for cooking

Method

1.   Put chicken, salt, water, and ground black pepper in the instant pot.

2.   Close and seal the lid and cook the chicken for 30 minutes on manual mode (high pressure). Make a quick pressure release.

3.   Meanwhile, spray the pan with cooking spray and heat it up. Add scallions and daikon and roast the vegetables for 5 minutes.

4.   Put the cooked vegetables in the round pan (pot pie pan).

5.   Add cooked chicken and heavy cream.

6.   Mix up Mozzarella, coconut flour, and eggs.

7.   Top the chicken with cheese mixture and bake in the oven for 20 minutes at 390F.

Nutritional info per serve: calories 202, fat 10.9, fiber 4.3, carbs 7.1, protein 18.6

Club Salad

Prep time: 15 minutes | **Cook time:** 25 minutes | **Yield:** 2 servings

Ingredients

½ cup butter leaves lettuce, chopped

1 oz bacon, chopped cooked

5 oz chicken fillet, chopped

1 avocado slice, chopped

1 tablespoon keto mayonnaise

1 cup water, for cooking

Method

1.   Pour water in the instant pot. Add chicken and cook it on manual mode (high pressure) for 25 minutes. Make a quick pressure release.

2.   Chop the cooked chicken and put it in the salad bowl.

3.   Add bacon, lettuce, avocado, and shake well.

4.   Sprinkle the salad with keto mayonnaise.

Nutritional info per serve: calories 237, fat 13.7, fiber 0.1, carbs 1.2, protein 25.9

TSO Chicken Drumsticks

Prep time: 10 minutes | **Cook time:** 20 minutes | **Yield:** 6 servings

Ingredients

6 chicken thighs

1 tablespoon apple cider vinegar

1 tablespoon coconut aminos

½ teaspoon ginger, grated

1 teaspoon Splenda

½ teaspoon chili flakes

¼ cup avocado oil

1/3 cup water

Method

1.   Heat up avocado oil on saute mode for 3 minutes and add chicken thighs.

2.   Saute the chicken for 6 minutes.

3.   Then add the rest of the ingredients and stir them gently.

4.   Close and seal the lid and cook the meal on Poultry mode for 10 minutes.

5.   Carefully stir the cooked chicken.

Nutritional info per serve: calories 179, fat 11.2, fiber 0.4, carbs 1.8, protein 19.1

Chicken&Cheddar Biscuits

Prep time: 15 minutes | **Cook time:** 10 minutes | **Yield:** 4 servings

Ingredients

3 oz chicken fillet, cooked, shredded

2 tablespoons almond flour

1 egg, beaten

½ teaspoon minced garlic

¼ cup coconut cream

3 oz Cheddar cheese, shredded

1 cup water, for cooking

Method

1.   In the mixing bowl, mix up shredded chicken, almond flour, egg, minced garlic, coconut cream, and shredded cheese.

2.   Then transfer the homogenous mixture in the muffin molds and flatten them gently with the help of the spoon.

3.   Pour water and insert the steamer rack in the instant pot.

4.   Place the muffin molds on the rack. Close and seal the lid.

5. Cook the meal on manual mode (high pressure) for 10 minutes. Allow the natural pressure release for 10 minutes.

Nutritional info per serve: calories 257, fat 20.3, fiber 1.8, carbs 4.3, protein 16.2

Bacon-Wrapped Tenders

Prep time: 15 minutes | **Cook time:** 15 minutes | **Yield:** 2 servings

Ingredients

4 oz chicken fillet

2 bacon slices

½ teaspoon ground paprika

¼ teaspoon salt

1 teaspoon olive oil

1 cup water, for cooking

Method

1. Cut the chicken fillet on 2 tenders and sprinkle them with salt, ground paprika, and olive oil.

2. Wrap the chicken tenders in the bacon and transfer in the steamer rack,

3. Pour water and insert the steamer rack with the chicken tenders in the instant pot.

4. Close and seal the lid and cook the meal on manual mode (high pressure) for 15 minutes.

5. When the time is finished, allow the natural pressure release for 10 minutes.

Nutritional info per serve: calories 232, fat 14.5, fiber 0.2, carbs 0.6, protein 23.5

Chicken Zucchini Rings

Prep time: 15 minutes | **Cook time:** 20 minutes | **Yield:** 2 servings

Ingredients

1 zucchini, trimmed

6 oz ground chicken

½ teaspoon chili flakes

½ teaspoon salt

½ teaspoon ginger paste

1 cup keto marinara sauce

Method

1. Slice the zucchini into the thick rings and remove the zucchini meat from the ring.

2. In the mixing bowl, mix up ground chicken, chili flakes, salt, and ginger paste.

3. Then fill the zucchini rings with chicken mixture and place them in the instant pot.

4. Add marinara sauce, close and seal the lid.

5. Cook the meal on manual mode (high pressure) for 20 minutes. Make a quick pressure release.

Nutritional info per serve: calories 203, fat 7.5, fiber 1.7, carbs 7.1, protein 26.3

Chicken Fritters

Prep time: 10 minutes | **Cook time:** 10 minutes | **Yield:** 4 servings

Ingredients

1 zucchini, grated

1 cup ground chicken

1 teaspoon chili powder

1 tablespoon avocado oil

1 egg, beaten

Method

1. Mix up zucchini, ground chicken, chili powder, and egg. When the mixture is smooth, make the medium size fritters.

2. Heat up the avocado oil in the instant pot on saute mode (appx. for 3 minutes).

3. Place the chicken fritters in the hot oil and cook them for 5 minutes per side.

Nutritional info per serve: calories 97, fat 4.3, fiber 0.9, carbs 2.3, protein 12.2

Chicken Carbonara

Prep time: 15 minutes | **Cook time:** 25minutes | **Yield:** 5 servings

Ingredients

1-pound chicken, skinless, boneless, chopped

1 cup heavy cream

1 cup spinach, chopped

2 oz Parmesan, grated

1 teaspoon ground black pepper

1 tablespoon coconut oil

2 oz bacon, chopped

Method

1. Put the coconut oil and chopped chicken in the instant pot.

2. Saute the chicken for 10 minutes. Stir it from time to time.

3. Then add ground black pepper, and spinach. Stir the mixture well and saute for 5 minutes more.

4. Then add heavy cream and Parmesan. Close and seal the lid.

5. Cook the meal on manual mode (high pressure) for 10 minutes. Allow the natural pressure release for 10 minutes.

Nutritional info per serve: calories 343, fat 21.6, fiber 0.2, carbs 1.7, protein 34.8

Crackle Chicken

Prep time: 10 minutes | **Cook time:** 30 minutes | **Yield:** 2 servings

Ingredients

2 chicken thighs

4 tablespoons butter

½ teaspoon white pepper

½ teaspoon salt

1 cup water, for cooking

Method

1. Pour water in the instant pot and add chicken thighs.

2. Close and seal the lid and cook the chicken for 20 minutes on manual mode (high pressure). Make a quick pressure release.

3. Remove the chicken and clean the instant pot.

4. Then toss the butter in the instant pot and melt it on saute mode.

5. Sprinkle the chicken thigs with salt and white pepper and add them in the melted butter.

6. Saute the chicken for 5 minutes per side.

Nutritional info per serve: calories 365, fat 33.1, fiber 0.1, carbs 0.4, protein 19.3

Marry Me Chicken

Prep time: 15 minutes | **Cook time:** 25 minutes | **Yield:** 4 servings

Ingredients

4 chicken thighs

1 teaspoon olive oil

1 teaspoon garlic, diced

1 teaspoon dried thyme

1 tablespoon avocado oil

¼ cup chicken broth

½ cup heavy cream

1 teaspoon salt

1 teaspoon ground black pepper

Method

1.   Pour olive oil in the instant pot and add chicken thighs.

2.   Saute them for 4 minutes from each side. Sprinkle the chicken with salt and ground black pepper.

3.   Then transfer the chicken on the plate.

4.   Add avocado oil in the instant pot.

5.   Then add dried thyme and garlic. Saute the ingredients for 2 minutes. Add chicken thighs, chicken broth, and heavy cream. Saute the chicken for 15 minutes.

Nutritional info per serve: calories 232, fat 17.3, fiber 0.4, carbs 1.4, protein 19.8

Chicken Divan

Prep time: 15 minutes | **Cook time:** 10 minutes | **Yield:** 4 servings

Ingredients

1 cup broccoli, chopped

2 tablespoons cream cheese

½ cup heavy cream

1 tablespoon curry powder

¼ cup chicken broth

½ cup Cheddar cheese, grated

6 oz chicken fillet, cooked chopped

Method

1.   Mix up broccoli and curry powder and put the mixture in the instant pot.

2.   Add heavy cream and cream cheese.

3.   Then add chicken and mix up the ingredients.

4.   Then add chicken broth and heavy cream.

5.   Top the mixture with Cheddar cheese. Close and seal the lid.

6.   Cook the meal on manual mode (high pressure) for 10 minutes. Allow the natural pressure release for 5 minutes, open the lid and cool the meal for 10 minutes.

Nutritional info per serve: calories 222, fat 15.5, fiber 1.1, carbs 3.2, protein 17.7

Tomato Chicken

Prep time: 10 minutes | **Cook time:** 35 minutes | **Yield:** 2 servings

Ingredients

2 chicken legs

2 tomatoes, chopped

1 cup chicken stock

1 teaspoon peppercorns

Method

1.   Put all ingredients in the instant pot.

2.	Close and seal the lid. Set "Manual" mode (high pressure).

3.	Cook the chicken legs for 35 minutes.

4.	Make a quick pressure release.

5.	Transfer the cooked chicken legs in the serving bowls and add 1 ladle of the chicken stock.

Nutritional info per serve: calories 294, fat 15.9, fiber 1.8, carbs 5.8, protein 31.1

Feta Chicken Drumsticks

Prep time: 7 minutes | **Cook time:** 15 minutes | **Yield:** 2 servings

Ingredients

4 lemon slices

2 chicken thighs

1 tablespoon Greek seasoning

4 oz Feta, crumbled

1 teaspoon butter

½ cup of water

Method

1.	Rub the chicken thighs with Greek seasoning.

2.	Then spread the chicken with butter.

3.	Pour water in the instant pot and place the trivet.

4.	Place the chicken on the foil and top with the lemon slices. Top it with Feta.

5.	Wrap the chicken in the foil and transfer on the trivet.

6.	Cook on the "Saute" mode for 10 minutes. Then make a quick pressure release for 5 minutes.

7.	Discard the foil from the chicken thighs and serve!

Nutritional info per serve: calories 341, fat 24.2, fiber 0.4, carbs 5.9, protein 27.5

White Mushrooms Poultry Stew

Prep time: 10 minutes | **Cook time:** 30 minutes | **Yield:** 2 servings

Ingredients

10 oz chicken breast, skinless, boneless

4 oz white mushrooms

¼ teaspoon salt

½ teaspoon white pepper

¾ teaspoon onion powder

½ teaspoon butter

¾ cup of water

1 tablespoon coconut cream

Method

1.	Chop the chicken breast roughly and place it in the instant pot bowl.

2.	Add salt, white pepper, onion powder, and water.

3.	Set the "Saute" mode and start to cook the poultry.

4.	Meanwhile, slice the mushrooms.

5.	Add chopped white mushrooms in the instant pot bowl.

6.	Add coconut cream and stir it.

7.	Close the lid and seal it. Set the timer for 25 minutes.

8.	Serve it!

Nutritional info per serve: calories 204, fat 6.5, fiber 0.9, carbs 3.4, protein 32.2

Celery Salad with Chicken

Prep time: 5 minutes | **Cook time:** 6 minutes |
Yield: 2 servings

Ingredients

1 cup celery, raw, diced

5 oz chicken breast, chopped

1 tablespoon butter

1 tablespoon lemon juice

½ teaspoon chili flakes

1 tablespoon fresh dill, chopped

½ tomato, chopped

¾ cup of water

Method

1.	Toss the butter in the instant pot and preheat it on the "Saute" mode.

2.	Add chopped chicken breast. Sprinkle it with the chili flakes and cook for 4 minutes.

3.	Add water and close the lid. Seal the lid and set the "Manual" mode + press timer for 3 minutes (High Pressure). Make the quick pressure release then.

4.	Add tomato and celery in the salad bowl.

5.	Add fresh dill and lemon juice.

6.	After this, add chicken breast (don't use the chicken water).

7.	Stir the salad directly before serving and enjoy!

Nutritional info per serve: calories 148, fat 7.8, fiber 1.3, carbs 3.2, protein 16

Indian Style Chicken

Prep time: 5 minutes | **Cook time:** 4 minutes |
Yield: 2 servings

Ingredients

¼ teaspoon cumin seeds

½ teaspoon turmeric

1 teaspoon ground paprika

¾ teaspoon chili paste

½ teaspoon ground coriander

½ cup of coconut milk

14 oz chicken breast, skinless, boneless

1 tablespoon coconut oil

Method

1.	Blend together the cumin seeds, turmeric, ground paprika, chili paste, coriander, coconut milk, and coconut oil.

2.	When the mixture is smooth – pour it in the instant pot bowl.

3.	Chop the chicken breast roughly and transfer it in the spice mixture. Stir gently with the help of the spatula.

4.	Lock the lid and seal it.

5.	Set the "Manual" mode for 4 minutes (High pressure).

6.	After this, make quick-release pressure.

7.	Enjoy!

Nutritional info per serve: calories 435, fat 26.6, fiber 1.9, carbs 5.1, protein 43.8

Marjoram Chicken Wings

Prep time: 7 minutes | **Cook time:** 10 minutes |
Yield: 2 servings

Ingredients

1 teaspoon marjoram

1 teaspoon cream cheese

½ green pepper

½ teaspoon salt

½ teaspoon ground black pepper

14 oz chicken wings

¾ cup of water

1 teaspoon coconut oil

Method

1. Rub the chicken wings with the marjoram, salt, and ground black pepper.

2. Blend the green pepper until you get a puree.

3. Rub the chicken wings in the green pepper puree.

4. Then toss the coconut oil in the instant pot bowl and preheat it on the "Saute" mode.

5. Add the chicken wings and cook them for 3 minutes from each side or until light brown.

6. Then add cream cheese and water.

7. Cook the meal on "Manual" mode and put the timer for 4 minutes + High Pressure.

8. When the time is over – make a quick pressure release.

9. Let the cooked chicken wings chill for 1-2 minutes and serve them!

Nutritional info per serve: calories 411, fat 17.7, fiber 0.8, carbs 1.9, protein 57.9

Chicken Cubes in Succulent Sauce

Prep time: 10 minutes | **Cook time:** 25 minutes | **Yield:** 2 servings

Ingredients

14 oz chicken breast

½ teaspoon ground cardamom

¼ teaspoon ground coriander

¾ teaspoon minced garlic

½ cup of coconut milk

½ teaspoon salt

¾ teaspoon nutmeg

1 teaspoon almond butter

Method

1. Mix up together the ground cardamom, ground coriander, minced garlic, and nutmeg.

2. Then chop the chicken breast roughly.

3. Stir the spice mixture in the full-fat cream and whisk until homogenous.

4. Place the almond butter and chicken in the instant pot bowl.

5. Add coconut milk and lock the instant pot lid.

6. Cook on the "Saute" mode for 25 minutes.

Nutritional info per serve: calories 421, fat 24.1, fiber 2.5, carbs 5.9, protein 45.3

Bacon Chicken

Prep time: 15 minutes | **Cook time:** 15 minutes | **Yield:** 3 servings

Ingredients

12 oz chicken breast, boneless, skinless

5 oz bacon, sliced

½ teaspoon cayenne pepper

½ teaspoon ground white pepper

½ teaspoon minced garlic

1 teaspoon salt

1 tablespoon butter

¾ cup of water

Method

1. Stir together cayenne pepper, ground white pepper, minced garlic, and salt.

2. Then beat the chicken breast with the help of the kitchen hammer gently. It will make the final taste of meat tender and juicy.

3. Pu the butter and bacon on it.

4. Roll up the chicken breast to make the roll.

5. Secure the chicken roll with the help of the kitchen twine.

6. Wrap the roll into the foil.

7. Pour 1 cup of water in the instant pot bowl and place the trivet.

8. Place the chicken roll on the trivet and close the lid.

9. Set the "Steam" mode and High pressure.

10. Cook the chicken roll for 15 minutes. Then use the natural pressure release method.

Nutritional info per serve: calories 421, fat 26.5, fiber 0.2, carbs 1.2, protein 41.7

Chicken Drumsticks de Provance

Prep time: 10 minutes | **Cook time:** 15 minutes | **Yield:** 2 servings

Ingredients

1 tablespoon herbs de Provance

4 chicken drumstick

¼ cup full-fat cream

1 teaspoon butter

Method

1. Rub the chicken drumstick with the herbs de Provance.

2. Melt the butter and mix it up with the full-fat cream.

3. Place the chicken drumstick on the foil and sprinkle with the creamy liquid.

4. Pour 1 cup of water in the instant pot and place the trivet there.

5. Transfer the chicken on the instant pot trivet.

6. Lock the instant pot lid and seal it.

7. Set the "Poultry" mode and timer for 15 minutes (High pressure).

8. When the poultry is cooked – use the quick pressure release method.

Nutritional info per serve: calories 192, fat 8.8, fiber 0, carbs 0.9, protein 25.6

Chicken Shish

Prep time: 10 minutes | **Cook time:** 5 minutes | **Yield:** 2 servings

Ingredients

1 tablespoon lemon juice

½ teaspoon cayenne pepper

½ teaspoon salt

10 oz chicken fillet

1 tablespoon avocado oil

Method

1. Chop the fillet into the medium cubes.

2. Sprinkle the chicken with the lemon juice, cayenne pepper, salt, and avocado oil.

3. Let it marinate for 10 minutes.

4. After this, string the ingredients on the skewers.

5. Place them in the baking pan.

6. Pour 1 cup of water in the instant pot and place trivet.

7. Transfer the baking pan in the instant pot, on the trivet. Sprinkle the chicken with the remaining oil mixture.

8. Lock the instant pot lid and set "Manual" mode (High Pressure).

9. Set timer for 5 minutes. After this, make a quick pressure release.

Nutritional info per serve: calories 282, fat 11.5, fiber 0.5, carbs 0.8, protein 41.2

Pecorino Chicken Cubes

Prep time: 10 minutes | **Cook time:** 15 minutes | **Yield:** 3 servings

Ingredients

2 oz Pecorino cheese, grated

10 oz chicken breast, skinless, boneless

1 tablespoon butter

¾ cup heavy cream

½ teaspoon salt

½ teaspoon red hot pepper

Method

1. Chop the chicken breast into the cubes.

2. Toss butter in the instant pot and preheat it on the "Saute" mode.

3. Add the chicken cubes.

4. Sprinkle the poultry with the salt and red hot pepper.

5. Add cream and mix up together all the ingredients.

6. Close the lid of the instant pot and seal it.

7. Set "Poultry" mode and put a timer on 15 minutes.

8. When the time is over – let the chicken rest for 5 minutes more.

9. Transfer the meal on the plates and sprinkle with the grated cheese. The cheese shouldn't melt immediately.

Nutritional info per serve: calories 340, fat 24.9, fiber 0, carbs 0.9, protein 28.3

Herbed Chicken Balls

Prep time: 10 minutes | **Cook time:** 15 minutes | **Yield:** 2 servings

Ingredients

10 oz chicken fillet

1 egg

1 tablespoon almond flour

¾ teaspoon salt

¾ teaspoon paprika

1 teaspoon thyme

½ teaspoon butter

¾ teaspoon dried dill

1 cup water, for cooking

Method

1. Chop the chicken fillet into the tiny pieces.

2. Mix up together the almond flour, thyme, and dried dill. Stir the mixture gently.

3. After this, combine together the chicken and almond flour mixture.

4. Stir it well and crack the egg in the mixture.

5. Mix it up until smooth.

6. Make the medium balls from the mixture.

7. Grease the instant pot pan with the butter and place the balls.

8. Add 1 cup of water and close the instant pot.

9. Set the "Manual" program (High pressure) for 8 minutes.

10. After this, make quick release and chill the balls little.

Nutritional info per serve: calories 336, fat 15.5, fiber 0.9, carbs 2.1, protein 44.8

Chicken with Almond Gravy

Prep time: 10 minutes | **Cook time:** 15 minutes | **Yield:** 2 servings

Ingredients

12 oz chicken breast, skinless, boneless

½ teaspoon salt

½ teaspoon white pepper

½ teaspoon ground black pepper

½ cup organic almond milk

½ teaspoon paprika

Method

1.   Mix up together salt, white pepper, ground black pepper, and paprika.

2.   Rub the chicken breast with the spice mixture generously.

3.   After this, place the chicken breast in the instant pot bowl.

4.   Add almond milk and close the lid.

5.   Set the "Poultry" program and cook the chicken for 8 minutes. NPR -5 minutes.

6.   Slice the chicken breast and sprinkle with the remaining gravy.

Nutritional info per serve: calories 112, fat 5, fiber 0.3, carbs 2.6, protein 36.5

Mexican Bowl

Prep time: 8 minutes | **Cook time:** 12 minutes | **Yield:** 3 servings

Ingredients

10 oz chicken fillet

5 oz avocado, cored

1 teaspoon butter

1 tablespoon Mexican style seasonings

3 tablespoons coconut milk

Method

1.   Cut the chicken fillet into the strips and sprinkle with the Mexican style seasonings.

2.   Place the chicken in the instant pot bowl and add butter and coconut milk.

3.   Set the "Poultry" program and cook it for 7 minutes (naturally release for 5 minutes).

4.   Meanwhile, slice avocado and place it into the serving bowls.

5.   Add the cooked chicken strips.

Nutritional info per serve: calories 329, fat 21.1, fiber 3.5, carbs 6.4, protein 28.6

Green Sandwich

Prep time: 10 minutes | **Cook time:** 10 minutes | **Yield:** 2 servings

Ingredients

4 oz kale leaves

8 oz chicken fillet

1 tablespoon butter

1 oz lemon

¼ cup of water

Method

1.   Dice the chicken fillet.

2.   Squeeze the lemon juice over the poultry.

3.   Transfer the poultry into the instant pot; add water and butter.

4.   Close the lid and cook the chicken on the "Poultry" mode for 10 minutes.

5.   When the chicken is cooked – place it on the kale leaves to make the medium sandwiches.

Nutritional info per serve: calories 298, fat 14.2, fiber 1.3, carbs.7.2, protein 34.7

Mini Chicken Hashes

Prep time: 15 minutes | **Cook time:** 7 minutes | **Yield:** 2 servings

Ingredients

2 oz scallions, chopped

¾ cup of water

1 teaspoon coconut milk

½ teaspoon almond butter

½ teaspoon ground black pepper

10 oz chicken fillet, diced

Method

1.   Set the "Stew" mode and toss the almond butter in the instant pot.

2.   When the almond butter is melted – add the diced chicken.

3.   Sprinkle it with the ground black pepper, chopped scallions, and add water.

4.   Add coconut milk.

5.   Close the lid and cook the meal for 7 minutes (High pressure).

6.   Make the natural pressure release for 10 minutes.

Nutritional info per serve: calories 310, fat 13.4, fiber 1.3, carbs 3.3, protein 42.5

Chicken with Adobo Peppers

Prep time: 15 minutes | **Cook time:** 12 minutes | **Yield:** 2 servings

Ingredients

4 chicken thighs

2 tablespoons chipotle peppers in Adobo sauce

½ cup of water

Method

1.   Pour water in the instant pot bowl.

2.   Add chicken thighs and chipotle peppers in Adobo sauce.

3.   Set the "Manual" mode (High pressure).

4.   Turn on the timer for 12 minutes.

5.   Make the natural pressure release for 10 minutes.

Nutritional info per serve: calories 326, fat 20.5, fiber 1, carbs 0.5, protein 38.5

Easy and Fast Chicken Drumsticks

Prep time: 10 minutes | **Cook time:** 10 minutes | **Yield:** 2 servings

Ingredients

4 chicken drumsticks

1 egg, whisked

½ teaspoon salt

1 tablespoon almond milk

1 tablespoon olive oil

1 cup water, for cooking

Method

1.   In the mixing bowl mix up chicken drumsticks, salt, almond milk, and whisked egg.

2.   Then massage the chicken with olive oil and transfer in the baking pan.

3.   Pour water in the instant pot. Insert the baking pan with chicken.

4.   Set the "Manual" mode and High pressure and cook the chicken for 10 minutes.

5.   Make a quick pressure release and open the lid.

Nutritional info per serve: calories 264, fat 16.2, fiber 0.2, carbs 0.6, protein 28.2

FISH AND SEAFOOD

Haddock under Spinach Blanket

Prep time: 15 minutes | **Cook time:** 15 minutes | **Yield:** 4 servings

Ingredients

12 oz haddock fillet

1 cup spinach

1 tablespoon avocado oil

1 teaspoon minced garlic

½ teaspoon ground coriander

1 cup water, for cooking

Method

1.   Blend the spinach until smooth and mix up with avocado oil, ground coriander, and minced garlic.

2.   Then cut the haddock into 4 fillets and place on the foil.

3.   Top the fish fillets with spinach mixture and place them on the rack.

4.   Pour water and insert the rack in the instant pot.

5.   Close and seal the lid and cook the haddock on manual (high pressure) for 15 minutes.

6.   Do the quick pressure release.

Nutritional info per serve: calories 103, fat 1.3, fiber 0.3, carbs 0.7, protein 20.9

Ginger Cod

Prep time: 10 minutes | **Cook time:** 20 minutes | **Yield:** 2 servings

Ingredients

1 teaspoon ginger paste

8 oz cod fillet, chopped

1 tablespoon coconut oil

¼ cup of coconut milk

Method

1.   Melt the coconut oil in the instant pot on saute mode.

2.   Then add ginger paste and coconut milk and bring the mixture to boil.

3.   Add chopped cod and saute the meal for 12 minutes. Stir the fish cubes with the help of the spatula from time to time.

Nutritional info per serve: calories 222, fat 15, fiber 0.8, carbs 2.3, protein 21

Salmon Pate

Prep time: 10 minutes | **Cook time:** 15 minutes | **Yield:** 6 servings

Ingredients

1-pound salmon

2 tablespoons cream cheese

½ teaspoon salt

1 teaspoon chives, chopped

1 cup water, for cooking

Method

1.   Put salmon and water in the instant pot.

2.   Close and seal the lid and cook the fish on manual (high pressure) mode for 15 minutes.

3.   Make a quick pressure release and transfer the salmon in the food processor.

4.   Add salt, chives, and cream cheese. Blend the fish mixture until smooth.

5.   Transfer the cooked pate in the glass jar.

Nutritional info per serve: calories 112, fat 5.8, fiber 0, carbs 0.1, protein 14.9

Mackerel Casserole

Prep time: 15 minutes | **Cook time:** 15 minutes | **Yield:** 5 servings

Ingredients

1 cup broccoli, shredded

10 oz mackerel, chopped

½ cup Cheddar cheese, shredded

1 cup of coconut milk

1 teaspoon ground cumin

1 teaspoon salt

Method

1.   Sprinkle the chopped mackerel with ground cumin and salt and transfer in the instant pot.

2.   Top the fish with shredded broccoli and Cheddar cheese,

3.   Then add coconut milk. Close and seal the lid.

4.   Cook the casserole on manual mode (high pressure) for 15 minutes.

5.   Allow the natural pressure release for 10 minutes and open the lid.

Nutritional info per serve: calories 312, fat 25.4, fiber 1.6, carbs 4.2, protein 18

Coconut Squid

Prep time: 10 minutes | **Cook time:** 20 minutes | **Yield:** 3 servings

Ingredients

1-pound squid, sliced

1 teaspoon tomato paste

1 cup of coconut milk

1 teaspoon cayenne pepper

½ teaspoon salt

Method

1.   Put all ingredients from the list above in the instant pot.

2.   Close and seal the lid and cook the squid on manual (high pressure) for 20 minutes.

3.   When the cooking time is finished, do the quick pressure release.

4.   Serve the squid with coconut milk gravy.

Nutritional info per serve: calories 326, fat 21.3, fiber 2, carbs 9.8, protein 25.5

Butter Scallops

Prep time: 10 minutes | **Cook time:** 10 minutes | **Yield:** 4 servings

Ingredients

1-pound sea scallops

1 tablespoon coconut aminos

¼ cup apple cider vinegar

1 garlic clove, diced

1 teaspoon chili flakes

¼ teaspoon salt

¼ cup butter

½ cup beef broth

Method

1.   Melt the butter on saute mode and add scallops.

2.   Cook them for 2 minutes per side.

3. Add all remaining ingredients. Close and seal the lid.

4. Cook the scallops on manual mode (high pressure) for 3 minutes. Allow the natural pressure release for 5 minutes.

Nutritional info per serve: calories 214, fat 12.5, fiber 0, carbs 4, protein 19.8

Fish Nuggets

Prep time: 15 minutes | **Cook time:** 9 minutes | **Yield:** 4 servings

Ingredients

1-pound tilapia fillet

½ cup almond flour

3 eggs, beaten

¼ cup avocado oil

1 teaspoon salt

Method

1. Cut the fish into the small pieces (nuggets) and sprinkle withs alt.

2. Then dip the fish nuggets in the eggs and coat in the almond flour.

3. Heat up avocado oil for 3 minutes on saute mode.

4. Put the prepared fish nuggets in the hot oil and cook them on saute mode for 3 minutes from each side or until they are golden brown.

Nutritional info per serve: calories 179, fat 7.8, fiber 1, carbs 1.8, protein 26.2

Cod Lime Pieces

Prep time: 10 minutes | **Cook time:** 9 minutes | **Yield:** 2 servings

Ingredients

6 oz cod fillet

1 teaspoon lime zest, grated

1 tablespoon lime juice

1 tablespoon coconut oil

1 egg, beaten

Method

1. Cut the cod fillet into medium cubes and sprinkle with lime juice and lime zest.

2. Then dip the fish cubes in the egg.

3. Heat up coconut oil on saute mode for 3 minutes.

4. Put the cod cubes in the hot oil in one layer and cook on saute mode for 4 minutes.

5. Then flip the on another side and cook for 2 minutes more.

Nutritional info per serve: calories 161, fat 9.8, fiber 0.1, carbs 0.9, protein 18

Crustless Fish Pie

Prep time: 15 minutes | **Cook time:** 15 minutes | **Yield:** 6 servings

Ingredients

1 cup cauliflower, boiled, mashed

3 eggs, hard-boiled, peeled, chopped

10 oz salmon, chopped, boiled

½ cup mozzarella cheese, shredded

½ cup heavy cream

¼ cup chicken broth

1 teaspoon salt

½ teaspoon ground paprika

Method

1. Mix up chopped salmon and eggs and transfer them in the instant pot bowl.

2. Sprinkle the mixture with salt and ground paprika.

3. After this, top it with mashed cauliflower and mozzarella.

4. Add chicken broth and heavy cream.

5. Close and seal the lid.

6. Cook the pie for 15 minutes on manual mode (high pressure). Make a quick pressure release.

Nutritional info per serve: calories 141, fat 9.3, fiber 0.5, carbs 1.6, protein 13.4

Lemon Halibut

Prep time: 10 minutes | **Cook time:** 9 minutes | **Yield:** 3 servings

Ingredients

3 halibut fillet

½ lemon, sliced

½ teaspoon white pepper

½ teaspoon ground coriander

1 tablespoon avocado oil

1 cup water, for cooking

Method

1. Pour water and insert the steamer rack in the instant pot.

2. Rub the fish fillets with white pepper, ground coriander, and avocado oil.

3. Place the fillets in the steamer rack.

4. Then top the halibut with sliced lemon. Close and seal the lid.

5. Cook the meal on High pressure for 9 minutes. Make a quick pressure release.

Nutritional info per serve: calories 328, fat 7.3, fiber 0.6, carbs 1.4, protein 60.7

Mozzarella Fish Sticks

Prep time: 15 minutes | **Cook time:** 7 minutes | **Yield:** 6 servings

Ingredients

10 oz cod fillet, grinded

1 egg, beaten

2 tablespoons flax meal

¼ cup Mozzarella, shredded

1 tablespoon coconut flakes

1/3 cup coconut oil

Method

1. In the mixing bowl, mix up grinded cod fillet, egg, and shredded Mozzarella.

2. Then mix up flax meal and coconut flakes.

3. After this, make the small sticks from the cheese mixture and coat them in the coconut flakes mixture.

4. Bring the coconut oil to boil on saute mode.

5. Put the fish sticks in the hot coconut oil and saute them for 2 minutes or until the sticks are light brown.

6. Dry the cooked mozzarella fish sticks with the paper towel.

Nutritional info per serve: calories 169, fat 14.6, fiber 0.7, carbs 0.9, protein 10.2

Flounder Meuniere

Prep time: 15 minutes | **Cook time:** 10 minutes | **Yield:** 4 servings

Ingredients

16 oz flounder fillet

½ teaspoon ground black pepper

½ teaspoon salt

½ cup almond flour

2 tablespoons olive oil

1 tablespoon lemon juice

1 teaspoon fresh parsley, chopped

Method

1. Cut the fish fillets into 4 servings and sprinkle with salt, ground black pepper, and lemon juice.

2. Heat up the instant pot on saute mode for 2 minutes and add olive oil.

3. Coat the flounder fillets in the almond flour and put them in the hot olive oil.

4. Saute the fish fillets for 4 minutes and then flip on another side.

5. Cook the meal for 3 minutes more or until it is golden brown.

6. Sprinkle the cooked flounder with the fresh parsley.

Nutritional info per serve: calories 214, fat 10.5, fiber 0.5, carbs 1, protein 28.2

Salmon Loaf

Prep time: 15 minutes | **Cook time:** 25 minutes | **Yield:** 6 servings

Ingredients

12 oz salmon, boiled, shredded

3 eggs, beaten

½ cup almond flour

1 teaspoon garlic powder

¼ cup parmesan, grated

1 teaspoon butter, softened

1 cup water, for cooking

Method

1. Pour water in the instant pot.

2. Mix up the rest of the ingredients in the mixing bowl and stir until smooth.

3. After this, transfer the salmon mixture in the loaf pan and flatten; insert the pan in the instant pot. Close and seal the lid.

4. Cook the meal on manual mode (high pressure) for 25 minutes.

5. When the cooking time is finished, make a quick pressure release and cool the loaf well before serving.

Nutritional info per serve: calories 172, fat 10.5, fiber 0.3, carbs 1.5, protein 18.9

Cod under the Bagel Spices Crust

Prep time: 10 minutes | **Cook time:** 10 minutes | **Yield:** 2 servings

Ingredients

6 oz cod fillet

1 tablespoon bagel spices

1 teaspoon olive oil

1 teaspoon butter

Method

1. Cut the cod fillet into 2 servings and sprinkle the bagel spices generously.

2. Then melt the butter in the instant pot. Add olive oil and stir gently.

3. Put the prepared cod fillets in the hot oil mixture and cook for 3.5 minutes per side on saute mode.

4.   After this, close the lid and cook the fish on saute mode for 3 minutes.

Nutritional info per serve: calories 133, fat 5, fiber 1.8, carbs 6.3, protein 16.7

Lobster Cakes

Prep time: 10 minutes | **Cook time:** 10 minutes | **Yield:** 6 servings

Ingredients

1-pound lobster meat, grinded

1 egg, beaten

2 oz scallions, chopped

¼ cup coconut flour

½ teaspoon chili flakes

3 tablespoons coconut oil

Method

1.   Heat up coconut oil for 2 minutes on saute mode.

2.   Meanwhile, mix up lobster meat, egg, scallions, coconut flour, and chili flakes. Make the medium size cakes and put them in the hot coconut oil.

3.   Saute the lobster cakes for 5 minutes per side or until they are golden brown.

Nutritional info per serve: calories 160, fat 9.4, fiber 2.3, carbs 5.5, protein 11.2

Flounder Baked with Artichokes

Prep time: 10 minutes | **Cook time:** 10 minutes | **Yield:** 2 servings

Ingredients

8 oz flounder fillet

1 lemon slice, chopped

1 teaspoon ground black pepper

¼ teaspoon salt

½ large artichoke, chopped

1 tablespoon sesame oil

1 cup water, for cooking

Method

1.   Brush the round baking pan with sesame oil.

2.   Then place the chopped artichoke in the baking pan and flatten it.

3.   Sprinkle the flounder fillet with ground black pepper and salt and put over the artichoke.

4.   Add chopped lemon.

5.   Pour water and insert the steamer rack in the instant pot.

6.   Place the pan with fish in the steamer. Close and seal the lid.

7.   Cook the meal on manual (high pressure) for 10 minutes. Make a quick pressure release.

Nutritional info per serve: calories 216, fat 8.6, fiber 2.6, carbs 5.3, protein 28.9

Mascarpone Tilapia

Prep time: 10 minutes | **Cook time:** 20 minutes | **Yield:** 2 servings

Ingredients

10 oz tilapia

½ cup mascarpone

1 garlic clove, diced

1 teaspoon ground nutmeg

1 tablespoon olive oil

½ teaspoon salt

Method

1.   Pour olive oil in the instant pot.

2. Add diced garlic and saute it for 4 minutes.

3. Add tilapia and sprinkle it with ground nutmeg. Saute the fish for 3 minutes per side.

4. Add mascarpone and close the lid.

5. Saute tilapia for 10 minutes.

Nutritional info per serve: calories 293, fat 16.7, fiber 0.3, carbs 2.9, protein 33.5

Tuna Stuffed Poblanos

Prep time: 15 minutes | **Cook time:** 12 minutes | **Yield:** 4 servings

Ingredients

7 oz tuna, canned, shredded

1 teaspoon cream cheese

¼ teaspoon minced garlic

2 oz Provolone cheese, grated

4 poblano pepper

1 cup water, for cooking

Method

1. Remove the seeds from poblano peppers.

2. In the mixing bowl, mix up shredded tuna, cream cheese, minced garlic, and grated cheese.

3. Then fill the peppers with tuna mixture and put it in the baking pan.

4. Pour water and insert the baking pan in the instant pot.

5. Cook the meal on manual mode (high pressure) for 12 minutes. Then make a quick pressure release.

Nutritional info per serve: calories 153, fat 8.1, fiber 1.3, carbs 2.2, protein 17.3

Salmon with Dill

Prep time: 7 minutes | **Cook time:** 8 minutes | **Yield:** 2 servings

Ingredients

1 teaspoon salt

2 tablespoons fresh dill, chopped

10 oz salmon fillet

¼ cup butter

½ cup of water

Method

1. Put butter and salt in the baking pan.

2. Add salmon fillet and dill. Cover the pan with foil.

3. Pour water in the instant pot and insert the baking pan with fish inside.

4. Set the "Steam" mode and cook the salmon for 8 minutes.

5. Unwrap the cooked salmon and serve!

Nutritional info per serve: calories 399, fat 31.9, fiber 0.4, carbs 1.8, protein 28.4

Cinnamon Prawns

Prep time: 5 minutes | **Cook time:** 6 minutes | **Yield:** 2 servings

Ingredients

1 teaspoon ground cinnamon

12 oz prawns

1 teaspoon butter

½ cup cream

Method

1. Set the "Saute" mode and toss the butter in the instant pot bowl. Melt it.

2.   Then add prawns and sprinkle them with the ground cinnamon.

3.   Stir well and cook for 3 minutes.

4.   After this, add cream and lock the instant pot lid. Cook the meal for 3 minutes (QR).

Nutritional info per serve: calories 260, fat 8.1, fiber 0.6, carbs 5.4, protein 39.3

Fish Cream Cheese Casserole

Prep time: 7 minutes | **Cook time:** 5 minutes | **Yield:** 2 servings

Ingredients

1 teaspoon chili flakes

10 oz tuna, chopped

½ teaspoon salt

2 tablespoons cream cheese

1 teaspoon coconut oil

Method

1.   Take the springform pan and grease it with the coconut oil.

2.   Make the layer of tuna in the springform pan.

3.   After this, put the layer of the cream cheese.

4.   Sprinkle the casserole with the salt and chili flakes.

5.   Top the casserole with the cream cheese.

6.   Pour 1 cup of water in the instant pot bowl and place the trivet.

7.   Put the casserole on the trivet and wrap it with the foil.

8.   Set "Manual" mode (High pressure) for 5 minutes -QPR.

9.   Chill the casserole little.

Nutritional info per serve: calories 318, fat 17.2, fiber 0, carbs 0.3, protein 38.4

Sour Seabass

Prep time: 5 minutes | **Cook time:** 3 minutes | **Yield:** 2 servings

Ingredients

14 oz seabass steak

1 tablespoon lemon juice

1 tablespoon apple cider vinegar

¾ teaspoon salt

¾ cup of coconut milk

½ teaspoon minced garlic

½ teaspoon smoked paprika

Method

1.   Mix up together the lemon juice, apple cider vinegar, salt, minced garlic, and smoked paprika.

2.   Rub the seabass steak with the spice mixture and place it in the instant pot bowl.

3.   Add coconut milk and lock the instant pot lid.

4.   Set the "Manual" mode for 3 minutes. Make the quick-release pressure then.

Nutritional info per serve: calories 619, fat 45.9, fiber 3.8, carbs 5.8, protein 47.3

Spicy Fish Balls

Prep time: 8 minutes | **Cook time:** 10 minutes | **Yield:** 3 servings

Ingredients

1 tablespoon butter

15 oz cod

¼ teaspoon dried oregano

1 teaspoon ground nutmeg

½ teaspoon dried dill

Method

1. Grind the cod and mix it up with all spices.

2. Heat up the butter on saute mode.

3. Make the small balls from the cod mixture and put them in the hot butter.

4. Cook the fish balls for 3 minutes from each side on saute mode.

Nutritional info per serve: calories 187, fat 5.4, fiber 0.2, carbs 0.5, protein 32.5

Haddock Bake

Prep time: 7 minutes | **Cook time:** 10 minutes | **Yield:** 2 servings

Ingredients

2 eggs, beaten

12 oz haddock fillet, chopped

1 tablespoon cream cheese

¾ teaspoon dried rosemary

2 oz Parmesan, grated

1 teaspoon butter

Method

1. Whisk the beaten eggs until homogenous. Add the cream cheese, dried rosemary, and dill.

2. Grease the springform with the butter and place the haddock inside.

3. Pour the egg mixture over the fish and add sprinkle with parmesan.

4. Set the "Manual" mode (High pressure) and cook for 5 minutes. Then make natural-release pressure for 5 minutes.

Nutritional info per serve: calories 380, fat 15.7, fiber 0.2, carbs 18, protein 56.3

Shrimp Ragout

Prep time: 5 minutes | **Cook time:** 8 minutes | **Yield:** 2 servings

Ingredients

½ cup of water

½ green pepper, chopped

1 teaspoon scallions, chopped

1 teaspoon turmeric

½ teaspoon salt

7 oz shrimps, peeled

¼ cup cauliflower, chopped

Method

1. Set "Saute" mode at instant pot.

2. When the "Hot" is displayed – pour water and inside.

3. Add all remaining ingredients.

4. Close the lid and change the "Saute" mode into "Manual" (High pressure).

5. Set the timer for 5 minutes.

6. When the time is over – use the quick pressure release method.

Nutritional info per serve: calories 131, fat 1.9, fiber 1.1, carbs 4.3, protein 23.2

Tender Salmon Fillets

Prep time: 10 minutes | **Cook time:** 10 minutes | **Yield:** 2 servings

Ingredients

1 tablespoon dried dill

10 oz salmon fillet (cut into 2 servings)

½ teaspoon salt

1 tablespoon cream cheese

1 tablespoon butter

Method

1.   Gently rub the fish fillets with dill and salt.

2.   Preheat the instant pot on the "Saute" mode until it is displayed "Hot".

3.   Toss the butter inside and melt it.

4.   Transfer the salmon fillets in the instant pot and cook them for 2 minutes from each side.

5.   Add the cream cheese and saute the fish for 4 minutes more.

Nutritional info per serve: calories 260, fat 16.3, fiber 0.2, carbs 1, protein 28.3

Steamed Seabass

Prep time: 5 minutes | **Cook time:** 8 minutes | **Yield:** 2 servings

Ingredients

10 oz seabass steak

1 teaspoon salt

1 teaspoon ground black pepper

1 cup water, for cooking

Method

1.   Rub the seabass steak with salt and ground black pepper.

2.   Pour water and insert the steamer rack in the instant pot.

3.   Place the fish on the rack. Close and seal the lid.

4.   Cook the fish on the "Steam" mode for 8 minutes (Quick pressure release).

Nutritional info per serve: calories 292, fat 17.4, fiber 1.4, carbs 0.7, protein 32.3

VEGAN

Keto Bread

Prep time: 15 minutes | **Cook time:** 30 minutes | **Yield:** 4 servings

Ingredients

4 eggs, beaten

1 teaspoon baking powder

1 cup almond flour

2 tablespoons chia seeds

1/3 cup coconut milk

1 teaspoon coconut oil, melted

1 cup of water

Method

1. Put all ingredients except water in the mixing bowl and knead the dough.

2. Then place the dough in the baking pan.

3. Pour water and insert the steamer rack in the instant pot.

4. Put the pan with dough on the steamer rack and close the lid.

5. Cook the bread on manual mode (high pressure) for 30 minutes.

6. Then make a quick pressure release.

7. Open the lid and let the cooked bread cool to room temperature.

8. Remove it from the pan and slice.

Nutritional info per serve: calories 322, fat 25.8, fiber 5.9, carbs 11, protein 13.2

Vegan Pepperoni

Prep time: 20 minutes | **Cook time:** 4 minutes | **Yield:** 6 servings

Ingredients

½ cup nutritional yeast

1 teaspoon smoked paprika

1 teaspoon garlic powder

½ teaspoon salt

½ cup coconut flour

1 tablespoon almond butter, melted

4 tablespoons water

1 cup water, for cooking

Method

1. Blend together nutritional yeast, smoked paprika, garlic powder, salt, coconut flour, almond butter, and 4 tablespoons of water.

2. Then transfer the mixture in the sausage link or foil bag. Make the shape of pepperoni. Secure the ends of the pepperoni.

3. Pour water in the instant pot.

4. Then place the pepperoni in the water.

5. Close and seal the lid.

6. Cook the meal on manual (high pressure) for 4 minutes.

7. Allow the natural pressure release for 10 minutes.

8. Then cool the cooked pepperoni well and slice it.

Nutritional info per serve: calories 106, fat 3.3, fiber 7.8, carbs 13.8, protein 8.2

Southern Okra

Prep time: 5 minutes | **Cook time:** 4 minutes |
Yield: 2 servings

Ingredients

½ teaspoon Erythritol

1 teaspoon almond flour

1 cup okra, sliced

1 teaspoon coconut oil

½ tomato, chopped

½ bell pepper, chopped

½ cup of water

Method

1.   Put all ingredients in the instant pot.

2.   Close and seal the lid.

3.   Then cook the meal on manual mode (high pressure) for 4 minutes.

4.   When the time is finished, make a quick pressure release and transfer the meal on the plates.

Nutritional info per serve: calories 60, fat 3.2, fiber 2.3, carbs 6.9, protein 1.7

Summer Squash Gratin

Prep time: 15 minutes | **Cook time:** 10 minutes | **Yield:** 4 servings

Ingredients

2 zucchinis, sliced

½ cup of coconut milk

3 oz tofu, shredded

1 teaspoon chili flakes

½ teaspoon dried dill

1 teaspoon coconut oil

1 cup water, for cooking

Method

1.   Grease the gratin mold with coconut oil.

2.   Then place the sliced zucchini inside.

3.   Add coconut milk, tofu, chili flakes, and dried dill.

4.   Cover the gratin with foil and place it on the steamer rack.

5.   Pour water in the instant pot.

6.   Then transfer the steamer rack with gratin in the instant pot and close the lid.

7.   Cook the gratin on manual mode (high pressure) for 10 minutes.

8.   When the time is finished, allow the natural pressure release for 10 minutes.

Nutritional info per serve: calories 110, fat 9.4, fiber 2, carbs 5.4, protein 3.7

Beet Hummus

Prep time: 10 minutes | **Cook time:** 35 minutes | **Yield:** 4 servings

Ingredients

8 oz beets, peeled

1 teaspoon tahini paste

½ teaspoon harissa

1 tablespoon lemon juice

2 tablespoons olive oil

½ teaspoon salt

2 cups of water

Method

1.   Put beets and water in the instant pot.

2.   Cook the vegetables on manual mode (high pressure) for 35 minutes.

3.   Then make a quick pressure release and open the lid.

4.   Chop the beets and put them in the blender.

5.   Add tahini paste, harissa, lemon juice, olive oil, and salt.

6.   Blend the mixture until smooth.

7.   Transfer the cooked hummus in the bowl.

Nutritional info per serve: calories 95, fat 7.9, fiber 1.3, carbs 6.2, protein 1.2

Scallions&Olives Salad

Prep time: 5 minutes | **Cook time:** 4 minutes | **Yield:** 2 servings

Ingredients

4 oz scallions, sliced

1 teaspoon coconut oil

½ teaspoon Splenda

½ cup olives, sliced

1 teaspoon sesame oil

1 tablespoon fresh parsley, chopped

Method

1.   Put the sliced scallions and coconut oil in the instant pot.

2.   Saute it for 4 minutes or until the scallions is light brown.

3.   Then transfer it in the salad bowl.

4.   Add sliced olives, parsley, and sesame oil. Stir the salad.

Nutritional info per serve: calories 102, fat 8.3, fiber 2.6, carbs 7.4, protein 1.4

Sesame Zoodle Salad

Prep time: 10 minutes | **Cook time:** 3 minutes | **Yield:** 6 servings

Ingredients

2 large zucchinis, trimmed

1 teaspoon sesame seeds

¼ teaspoon chili flakes

1 tablespoon coconut aminos

¼ cup chicken broth

1 teaspoon sesame oil

1 tablespoon scallions, chopped

Method

1.   Make the noodles from the zucchini using the spiralizer.

2.   Then put them in the instant pot and add chicken broth.

3.   Saute the zucchini zoodles for 3 minutes and transfer in the serving bowls.

4.   Sprinkle the meal with sesame seeds, chili flakes, coconut aminos, sesame oil, and scallions.

5.   Gently stir the zoodles.

Nutritional info per serve: calories 31, fat 1.3, fiber 1.3, carbs 4.3, protein 1.6

Broccoli Rice Bowl

Prep time: 10 minutes | **Cook time:** 1 minute | **Yield:** 2 servings

Ingredients

1 ½ cup broccoli, shredded

½ teaspoon salt

½ teaspoon ground turmeric

2 tablespoons cream cheese

1 cup water, for cooking

Method

1.   Pour water and insert the steamer rack in the instant pot.

2. Put the broccoli shred in the bowl and transfer it in the steamer rack.

3. Close and seal the lid and cook it on manual mode (high pressure) for 1 minute + quick pressure release.

4. Transfer the cooked broccoli in the bowl and add salt, turmeric, and cream cheese.

5. Stir it well.

Nutritional info per serve: calories 60, fat 3.8, fiber 1.9, carbs 5.2, protein 2.7

Low Carb Budha Bowl

Prep time: 10 minutes | **Cook time:** 5 minutes | **Yield:** 2 servings

Ingredients

½ cup cauliflower, chopped

½ cup mushrooms, chopped

4 oz bok choy, chopped

1 tablespoon avocado oil

½ teaspoon salt

1 tablespoon lemon juice

1 cup water, for cooking

Method

1. Pour water and insert the steamer in the instant pot.

2. Put all vegetables in the steamer; close and seal the lid.

3. Cook the ingredients on steam mode for 5 minutes. Then do the quick pressure release.

4. After this, transfer the cooked vegetables in the serving bowls and sprinkle with salt, lemon juice, and avocado oil.

Nutritional info per serve: calories 29, fat 1.1, fiber 1.7, carbs 3.7, protein 2.1

Falafel Salad

Prep time: 20 minutes | **Cook time:** 10 minutes | **Yield:** 4 servings

Ingredients

2 cups lettuce, chopped

1 cucumber, chopped

1 tablespoon olive oil

1 teaspoon lemon juice

½ teaspoon cayenne pepper

1 cup cauliflower, shredded

1 egg, beaten

1/3 cup coconut flour

1 teaspoon lemon zest, grated

2 tablespoons coconut oil

Method

1. Make the falafel: mix up grated lemon zest, coconut flour, egg, and cauliflower.

2. Then make the small balls (falafel).

3. Melt the coconut oil in the instant pot on saute mode and add falafel. Place them in one layer,

4. Cook the falafel balls on saute mode for 3-4 minutes per side or until they are golden brown.

5. Meanwhile, in the salad bowl, mix up lettuce, cucumber, olive oil, lemon juice, and cayenne pepper. Shake the salad well.

6. Then top it with the cooked falafel.

Nutritional info per serve: calories 174, fat 13.3, fiber 5.3, carbs 11.2, protein 4.6

Portobello Steak

Prep time: 7 minutes | **Cook time:** 10 minutes | **Yield:** 2 servings

Ingredients

7 oz Portobello mushroom cap

1 teaspoon butter

¼ teaspoon meat seasonings

¼ cup ricotta cheese

Method

1.   Rub the mushrooms with meat seasonings and put in the instant pot.

2.   Add butter and cook the vegetables on saute mode for 3 minutes from each side.

3.   Then add ricotta cheese and cook mushroom steaks for 4 minutes more.

Nutritional info per serve: calories 85, fat 4.6, fiber 1.5, carbs 6.6, protein 6

Zucchini Hasselback

Prep time: 15 minutes | **Cook time:** 8 minutes | **Yield:** 2 servings

Ingredients

2 zucchinis, trimmed

2 teaspoons olive oil

½ teaspoon white pepper

½ teaspoon salt

1 cup water, for cooking

Method

1.   Cut the zucchinis in the shape of the Hasselback and sprinkle with white pepper, salt, and olive oil.

2.   Then place the vegetables on the rack and place it in the instant pot. Add water.

3.   Close and seal the lid and cook the meal on manual mode (high pressure) for 8 minutes.

4.   Make a quick pressure release and remove the zucchinis from the instant pot.

Nutritional info per serve: calories 73, fat 5, fiber 2.3, carbs 6.9, protein 2.4

Portobello Cheese Sandwiches

Prep time: 15 minutes | **Cook time:** 6 minutes | **Yield:** 2 servings

Ingredients

4 Portobello mushrooms caps

¼ teaspoon minced garlic

1 tablespoon olive oil

2 Cheddar cheese slices

1 cup water, for cooking

Method

1.   In the shallow bowl mix up garlic and olive oil.

2.   Brush the mushrooms with garlic mixture and place them on the trivet.

3.   Pour water in the instant pot. Transfer the trivet with mushroom caps inside.

4.   Close and seal the lid and cook the vegetables for 6 minutes on manual mode (high pressure).

5.   Then make a quick pressure release and open the lid.

6.   Place the cheese slices on 2 mushroom caps and cover them with remaining mushroom to get the shape of sandwiches.

Nutritional info per serve: calories 188, fat 16.3, fiber 0, carbs 1.9, protein 8.4

Turnip Roast

Prep time: 10 minutes | **Cook time:** 10 minutes | **Yield:** 2 servings

Ingredients

2 turnips, peeled, chopped

½ teaspoon ground paprika

1 tablespoon olive oil

¼ teaspoon salt

¼ teaspoon ground black pepper

Method

1.   Sprinkle the chopped turnip with ground paprika, salt, and ground black pepper.

2.   Then heat up olive oil in the instant pot on saute mode and add chopped turnip.

3.   Cook the turnip on saute mode for 3 minutes from each side.

4.   Then close the lid and saute it for 4 minutes more.

Nutritional info per serve: calories 97, fat 7.1, fiber 2.3, carbs 8.5, protein 1.1

Butter Chanterelle Mushrooms

Prep time: 10 minutes | **Cook time:** 15 minutes | **Yield:** 4 servings

Ingredients

14 oz chanterelle mushrooms, chopped

½ cup heavy cream

3 tablespoons butter

1 teaspoon salt

½ teaspoon dried thyme

Method

1.   Melt the butter in the instant pot on saute mode and add chanterelle mushrooms.

2.   Add dried thyme and salt and saute the vegetables for 5 minutes.

3.   Then stir them well and add heavy cream. Close and seal the lid.

4.   Cook the mushrooms on manual mode (high pressure) for 10 minutes.

5.   Then do the quick pressure release.

Nutritional info per serve: calories 130, fat 14.2, fiber 0.1, carbs 0.7, protein 0.6

DESSERTS

Lime Mugs

Prep time: 15 minutes | **Cook time:** 15 minutes | **Yield:** 2 servings

Ingredients

½ cup of coconut milk

½ teaspoon lime zest, grated

1/3 teaspoon baking powder

4 tablespoons almond flour

1 egg yolk

1 tablespoon liquid stevia

1 cup water (for instant pot)

Method

1. Whisk the coconut milk gently and add lime zest.

2. Add baking powder and almond flour.

3. After this, whisk the egg and add it to the coconut mixture. Add liquid stevia.

4. Whisk the mixture until smooth and pour it into the mugs.

5. Cover the top of the mugs with the foil and make the small holes with the help of the toothpick.

6. Pour water into the instant pot and insert the steamer rack.

7. Seal the lid and set the "steam" mode.

8. Cook the cakes on "steam" mode for 13 minutes + quick pressure release.

9. Chill the cakes for 5 minutes and discard the foil.

Nutritional info per serve: calories 250, fat 23.2, fiber 2.9, carbs 7.1, protein 5.7

Spiced Pudding

Prep time: 10 minutes | **Cook time:** 30 minutes | **Yield:** 2 servings

Ingredients

1 egg, beaten

¼ cup heavy cream

1 tablespoon Erythritol

¼ teaspoon pumpkin pie spices

1 teaspoon coconut oil

1 cup of water (for instant pot)

Method

1. Whisk the egg and mix it up with the heavy cream.

2. Add Erythritol and pumpkin pie spices. Stir the mixture.

3. Grease the cake pan with the coconut oil and transfer the pudding mixture inside.

4. Pour 1 cup of water in the instant pot.

5. Put the pudding on the steamer rack in the instant pot.

6. Cover the pudding with the foil and secure edges.

7. Put the "Manual" mode (High pressure) for 20 minutes.

8. Make the natural pressure release for 10 minutes.

9. Chill the pudding for 10 hours before serving.

Nutritional info per serve: calories 101, fat 10, fiber 0, carbs 8.2, protein 3.1

Coconut Balls

Prep time: 5 minutes | **Cook time:** 8 minutes | **Yield:** 2 servings

Ingredients

2 tablespoon coconut flakes

1 egg, whisked

2 tablespoons coconut flour

¾ teaspoon vanilla extract

1 teaspoon Erythritol

1 tablespoon coconut oil

1 cup of water (for instant pot)

Method

1.   Combine together the whisked egg, coconut flour, coconut flakes, and vanilla extract. Add coconut oil.

2.   Add baking powder and Erythritol.

3.   Make the balls from the coconut flour mixture.

4.   Pour 1 cup of water in the instant pot.

5.   Insert the steamer rack inside and place the ramekin on it. Add coconut balls.

6.   Close and lock the instant pot lid.

7.   Set the "Manual" mode for 8 minutes – high pressure. QPR

8.   Chill the dessert for 5-10 minutes or until they are warm.

Nutritional info per serve: calories 142, fat 11.4, fiber 3.5, carbs 6.8, protein 3.9

Turnip Cake Cups

Prep time: 15 minutes | **Cook time:** 10 minutes | **Yield:** 2 servings

Ingredients

1 egg

1 tablespoon butter

1 teaspoon liquid stevia

¾ teaspoon vanilla extract

½ cup turnip, chopped

1 tablespoon macadamia nuts, crushed

¾ 2 tablespoons coconut flour

¾ teaspoon ground cinnamon

¾ teaspoon baking powder

1 cup of water (for instant pot)

Method

1.   Crack the egg in the mixing bowl and whisk it well with the help of the hand whisker.

2.   Add liquid stevia, vanilla extract, coconut flour, ground cinnamon, and baking powder.

3.   Stir well until smooth.

4.   Then add macadamia nuts and turnip.

5.   Mix up the batter with the help of the spoon until homogenous.

6.   Pour the batter into the non-stick cake molds.

7.   Then pour 1 cup of water in the instant pot. Insert the steamer rack.

8.   Transfer the cakes on the rack and close the instant pot lid.

9.   Seal the lid and set the "Manual" mode (High pressure) for 10 minutes. (QPR).

10.   Chill the cakes for 10-15 minutes

Nutritional info per serve: calories 147, fat 11.3, fiber 4.5, carbs 9.3, protein 4.5

Ramekin Red Cakes

Prep time: 10 minutes | **Cook time:** 15 minutes | **Yield:** 2 servings

Ingredients

¼ teaspoon red food coloring

2 teaspoons almond butter

¼ teaspoon baking powder

1 teaspoon lemon juice

4 tablespoons almond flour

3 tablespoons coconut cream

1 cup water, for cooking

Method

1.   Mix up red food coloring, almond butter, baking powder, lemon juice, and almond flour.

2.   Add coconut cream.

3.   Stir the mixture until it is smooth.

4.   After this, pour the mixture in the non-sticky ramekins.

5.   Pour water and insert the steamer rack in the instant pot.

6.   Place the ramekins on the rack. Cook the muffins on manual (high pressure) for 15 minutes + quick pressure release.

Nutritional info per serve: calories 235, fat 21, fiber 3.6, carbs 7.6, protein 6.9

Avocado Bread

Prep time: 5 minutes | **Cook time:** 3 minutes | **Yield:** 4 servings

Ingredients

1 avocado, mashed

½ teaspoon baking powder

¼ teaspoon apple cider vinegar

1 teaspoon vanilla extract

1 tablespoon Erythritol

1 egg, whisked

¼ cup coconut cream

½ cup coconut flour

1 cup water (for instant pot)

Method

1.   Combine together the baking powder, apple cider vinegar, vanilla extract, Erythritol, and whisked egg.

2.   Add coconut cream and coconut flour.

3.   Add mashed avocado.

4.   Mix up the mixture until you get the homogenous texture.

5.   Transfer the dough into the non-stick cake mold and flatten gently with the help of the spatula.

6.   Wrap the mold in the aluminum foil.

7.   Pour water in the instant pot and insert the steamer rack. Place the mold on the rack and close the lid.

8.   Cook the bread on the "Steam" mode for 20 minutes. Use the quick pressure release.

9.   Chill the bread and remove it from the cake mold.

Nutritional info per serve: calories 216, fat 16, fiber 9.7, carbs 19.4, protein 4.7

Nutmeg and Cinnamon Cake

Prep time: 15 minutes | **Cook time:** 10 minutes | **Yield:** 4 servings

Ingredients

1 teaspoon ground nutmeg

½ teaspoon ground cinnamon

1 egg, whisked

1/3 teaspoon baking powder

½ cup coconut flour

1 tablespoon almond butter

¼ cup of water

1 cup water (for instant pot)

Method

1. Stir together the whisked egg and water.

2. Add almond butter, coconut flour, baking powder, ground cinnamon, and ground nutmeg.

3. Stir the mixture together until smooth and homogenous.

4. Transfer the dough into the non-stick cake pan and flatten it well with the help of the fingertips.

5. Pour 1 cup of water in the instant pot bowl and insert the trivet.

6. Put the cake pan on the trivet and cover it with the foil.

7. Coo the cake on "Manual" mode (High pressure) for 10 minutes + NPR.

Nutritional info per serve: calories 104, fat 5, fiber 6.7, carbs 11.5, protein 4.3

Vanilla Curd

Prep time: 5 minutes | **Cook time:** 5 minutes | **Yield:** 3 servings

Ingredients

4 egg yolks, whisked

2 tablespoon butter

1 tablespoon Erythritol

½ cup organic almond milk

1 teaspoon vanilla extract

Method

1. Set the instant pot in "Saute" mode and when the "Hot" is displayed – add butter.

2. Melt the butter but not boil it and add whisked egg yolks, almond milk, and vanilla extract.

3. Add Erythritol. Whisk the mixture.

4. Cook the meal on "Low" for 6 hours.

Nutritional info per serve: calories 154, fat 14.1, fiber 0, carbs 7.3, protein 3.9

Mint Brownies

Prep time: 20 minutes | **Cook time:** 10 minutes | **Yield:** 4 servings

1 tablespoon cocoa powder

1 tablespoon Erythritol

2 egg yolks, whisked

¼ cup of coconut milk

1 teaspoon butter

1 teaspoon dried mint

3 tablespoons almond flour, gluten-free

1 cup of water (for instant pot)

Method

1. Pour coconut milk in the instant pot bowl and start to cook it on "saute" mode.

2. Add cocoa powder.

3. After this, add coconut milk and butter.

4. When the mixture is smooth – start to add whisked egg yolks gradually. Add almond flour.

5. Whisk the mixture without stopping.

6. Add Erythritol and mint. Whisk it all the time. Then flatten it.

7. Cook the dessert on "manual" mode for 10 minutes (QPR for 5 minutes).

8. Cut the dessert into bars.

Nutritional info per serve: calories 196, fat 17.8, fiber 3, carbs 10.3, protein 6.6

Pancake Bites

Prep time: 10 minutes | **Cook time:** 10 minutes | **Yield:** 4 servings

Ingredients

1 teaspoon apple cider vinegar

1 teaspoon vanilla extract

1 cup of coconut milk

1/3 cup coconut flour

1 tablespoon Erythritol

½ teaspoon baking powder

1 tablespoon coconut oil

Method

1.   Melt the almond butter on saute mode.

2.   Then mix up all the remaining ingredients in the mixing bowl.

3.   Pour the small amount of pancake batter in the instant pot to get the small rounds.

4.   Cook the pancake bites on saute mode for 1.5 minutes from each side.

Nutritional info per serve: calories 211, fat 18.7, fiber 5.3, carbs 14.2, protein 2.7

Fluffy Brulee

Prep time: 10 minutes | **Cook time:** 9 minutes | **Yield:** 3 servings

Ingredients

1 cup coconut cream

4 egg yolks

2 teaspoons Erythritol

1 cup of water (for instant pot)

Method

1.   Whisk the egg yolk until you get the yellow color.

2.   Then add coconut cream and keep whisking the egg yolk mixture until smooth.

3.   Add 1 teaspoon of Erythritol. Stir it well and transfer into the ramekins.

4.   Pour 1 cup of water in the instant pot bowl. Place the steamer rack inside the instant pot.

5.   Transfer the ramekins on the rack and wrap the top of ramekins with the foil.

6.   Set the "Manual" mode (High pressure) and cook the dessert for 9 minutes.

7.   Allow the natural pressure release for 15 minutes.

8.   Chill the dessert for 2 hours.

Nutritional info per serve: calories 256, fat 25.1, fiber 1.8, carbs 8.6, protein 5.4

Mug Muffins

Prep time: 10 minutes | **Cook time:** 8 minutes | **Yield:** 3 servings

Ingredients

1 teaspoon avocado oil

2 tablespoons coconut flour

1 tablespoon Erythritol

½ teaspoon vanilla extract

¼ teaspoon baking powder

1 tablespoon almond butter

1 cup of water (for instant pot)

Method

1.   Brush the mugs with avocado oil

2.   Mix up together all remaining the liquid ingredients and almond butter.

3.   Add all the dry ingredients and stir the mixture with the help of the spoon.

4. When you get a smooth batter – transfer it into the prepared mugs.

5. Pour 1 cup of water in the instant pot and insert the steamer rack.

6. Put the mugs on the rack and close the lid.

7. Cook the meal on "Manual" (High pressure) for 8 minutes. QPR for 5 minutes.

Nutritional info per serve: calories 58, fat 3.7, fiber 2.6, carbs 9.4, protein 2.3

Pecan Bites

Prep time: 20 minutes | **Cook time:** 8 minutes | **Yield:** 4 servings

Ingredients

2 pecans, crushed

1 tablespoon coconut oil, softened

1 egg, whisked

½ cup almond flour

1 tablespoon Erythritol

½ teaspoon vanilla extract

¼ cup of coconut milk

¾ teaspoon ground cinnamon

½ teaspoon sesame oil

Method

1. Spread the non-sticky springform mold with the sesame oil.

2. Then combine together the softened coconut oil, whisked egg, almond flour, vanilla extract, coconut milk, Erythritol, and ground cinnamon. Add pecans.

3. Check if all the ingredients are added and mix up the mixture until smooth.

4. Transfer the mixture in the prepared springform pan and flatten it well.

5. Place the pan in the instant pot and cover with the foil.

6. Close the lid and cook the dessert on the "Manual" mode for 8 minutes (follow the directions of your instant pot). NPR for 15 minutes.

7. Cut the meal into bites.

Nutritional info per serve: calories 220, fat 20.3, fiber 2.8, carbs 9, .1protein 5.5

Sweet Zucchini Crisps

Prep time: 6 minutes | **Cook time:** 8 minutes | **Yield:** 2 servings

Ingredients

1 tablespoon Erythritol

1 zucchini

1 tablespoon butter

Method

1. Slice the zucchini into thin rounds.

2. The heat up butter on saute mode. When the butter is hot, add zucchini slices and cook them for 4 minutes from each side or until they become light crispy.

3. Then sprinkle the cooked crisps with Erythritol and put on the paper towel for 10 minutes to cool.

Nutritional info per serve: calories 67, fat 5.9, fiber 1.1, carbs 3.3, protein 1.3

Sugar-Free Coconut Squares

Prep time: 15 minutes | **Cook time:** 4 minutes | **Yield:** 2 servings

Ingredients

1/3 cup coconut flakes

1 tablespoon butter

1 egg, beaten

1 cup water, for cooking

Method

1.   Mix up together coconut flakes, butter, and egg.

2.   Then put the mixture into the square shape mold and flatten well.

3.   Pour water and insert the steamer rack in the instant pot.

4.   Put the mold with dessert on the rack. Close and seal the lid.

5.   Cook the meal on manual mode (high pressure) for 4 minutes. Make a quick pressure release.

6.   Cool the cooked dessert little and cut into the squares.

Nutritional info per serve: calories 130, fat 12.4, fiber 1.2, carbs 2.2, protein 3.3

Custard Tarts

Prep time: 10 minutes | **Cook time:** 20 minutes | **Yield:** 2 servings

Ingredients

¼ cup almond flour

1 tablespoon coconut oil

2 egg yolks

¼ cup of coconut milk

1 tablespoon Erythritol

1 teaspoon vanilla extract

1 cup water, for cooking

Method

1.   Make the dough: mix up almond flour and coconut oil.

2.   Then place the dough into 2 mini tart molds and flatten well in the shape of cups.

3.   Pour water in the instant pot. Insert the steamer rack.

4.   Place the tart mold in the instant pot. Close and seal the lid.

5.   Cook them for 3 minutes on Manual mode (high pressure). Make a quick pressure release.

6.   Then whisk together vanilla extract, Erythritol, coconut milk, and egg yolks.

7.   Pour the liquid in the tart molds and close the lid.

8.   Cook the dessert for 7 minutes on manual mode (high pressure).

9.   Then allow the natural pressure release for 10 minutes more.

Nutritional info per serve: calories 208, fat 20.2, fiber 1, carbs 3.3, protein 4.1

Peanut Cheesecake

Prep time: 10 minutes | **Cook time:** 8 hours | **Yield:** 4 servings

Ingredients

1 cup cream cheese

4 eggs, beaten

1 teaspoon vanilla extract

¼ cup of coconut milk

1 teaspoon coconut oil

1 tablespoon erythritol

2 oz peanuts, chopped

1 cup water, for cooking

Method

1. Mix up together cream cheese, eggs, vanilla extract, coconut milk, coconut oil, Erythritol, and peanuts.

2. Then pour the liquid in the instant pot baking pan. Flatten the surface of the cheesecake if desired.

3. Then pour water in the instant pot and insert the mold with cheesecake.

4. Close the lid and cook the dessert on "low" mode for 8 hours.

Nutritional info per serve: calories 393, fat 6.3, fiber 1.5, carbs 8.9, protein 13.9

Cardamom Rolls

Prep time: 20 minutes | **Cook time:** 18 minutes | **Yield:** 5 servings

Ingredients

½ cup coconut flour

1 tablespoon ground cardamom

2 tablespoon Splenda

1 egg, whisked

¼ cup almond milk

1 tablespoon butter, softened

1 tablespoon cream cheese

1/3 cup of water (for instant pot)

Method

1. Combine together coconut flour, almond milk, and softened butter.

2. Knead the smooth dough.

3. Roll up the dough with the help of the rolling pin.

4. Then combine together Erythritol and ground cardamom.

5. Sprinkle the surface of the dough with the ground cardamom mixture.

6. Roll the dough into one big roll and cut them into servings.

7. Place the rolls into the instant pot round mold.

8. Pour water in the instant pot (1/3 cup) and insert the mold inside.

9. Set "Manual" mode (High pressure) for 18 minutes.

10. Then use the natural pressure release method for 15 minutes.

11. Chill the rolls to the room temperature and spread with cream cheese.

Nutritional info per serve: calories 128, fat 5.9, fiber 4.5, carbs 12.5, protein 5

Keto Soufflé

Prep time: 10 minutes | **Cook time:** 6 hours | **Yield:** 4 servings

Ingredients

½ cup of coconut milk

4 egg yolks

2 tablespoons Splenda

1 tablespoon almond flour

1 cup of water (for instant pot)

Method

1. Put coconut milk, egg yolk, Splenda, and almond flour in the blender.

2. Blend the mixture until smooth and pour it in the small ramekins.

3. Then pour water in the instant pot and place the ramekins with soufflé inside.

4. Close the lid and cook the dessert on "Low" for 6 hours.

Nutritional info per serve: calories 163, fat 12.5, fiber 0.9, carbs 8.7, protein 3.8

Zebra Cakes in Cup

Prep time: 8 minutes | **Cook time:** 10 minutes | **Yield:** 3 servings

Ingredients

1 egg, whisked

2 tablespoons butter, melted

1 teaspoon Splenda

4 tablespoons almond flour

1 tablespoon cocoa powder

1 cup of water (for instant pot)

Method

1. Mix up egg, butter, Splenda, and almond flour. Whisk the mixture until smooth.

2. Then separate the liquid into halves.

3. Pour white liquid into the baking cups.

4. Add the cocoa in the remaining white batter and whisk until it turns the color into chocolate.

5. Add the chocolate liquid in the baking cups too and gently stir to get the zebra stripes.

6. Pour 1 cup of water in the instant pot. Place the steamer rack.

7. Transfer the cups on the steamer rack and close the lid.

8. Seal the instant pot lid and set the "Manual" mode.

9. Put the timer for 9 minutes (Quick pressure release).

10. When the dessert is cooked – let it chill for 1 hour.

Nutritional info per serve: calories 313, fat 28.1, fiber 4.5, carbs 10.4, protein 10.3

Frozen Strawberry Cheesecake

Prep time: 20 minutes | **Cook time:** 10 minutes | **Yield:** 2 servings

Ingredients

1 tablespoon gelatin

4 tablespoon water (for gelatin)

4 tablespoon cream cheese

1 strawberry, chopped

¼ cup of coconut milk

1 tablespoon swerve

Method

1. Mix up gelatin and water and leave the mixture for 10 minutes.

2. Meanwhile, pour coconut milk in the instant pot.

3. Bring it to boil on saute mode (appx. For 10 minutes).

4. Meanwhile, mash the strawberry and mix it up with cream cheese.

5. Add the mixture in the hot coconut milk and stir until smooth.

6. Cool the liquid for 10 minutes and add gelatin. Whisk it until gelatin is melted.

7. Then pour the cheesecake in the mold and freeze in the freezer for 3 hours.

Nutritional info per serve: calories 155, fat 14.1, fiber 0.8, carbs 3.7, protein 5.2

Avocado Muffins

Prep time: 15 minutes | **Cook time:** 10 minutes | **Yield:** 3 servings

Ingredients

2 tablespoons almond flour

1 teaspoon flax meal

2 teaspoon swerve

¼ teaspoon baking powder

3 tablespoons coconut milk

2 eggs, beaten

½ avocado, mashed

1 cup of water (for instant pot)

Method

1.   Whisk together the beaten egg, coconut milk, and baking powder.

2.   Add swerve and flax meal.

3.   After this, add almond flour, mashed avocado, and stir until homogenous.

4.   Pour the batter into the muffin molds.

5.   Pour 1 cup of water in the instant pot and insert the steamer ramekin.

6.   Transfer the muffins on the rack.

7.   Set the "Manual" mode and put the timer on 10 minutes (High Pressure – QR for 10 minutes).

8.   Cool the muffins to the room temperature.

Nutritional info per serve: calories 259, fat 22.6, fiber 4.8, carbs 9.7, protein 8.8

Vanilla Liquid Cake

Prep time: 15 minutes | **Cook time:** 5 minutes | **Yield:** 2 servings

Ingredients

¼ teaspoon vanilla extract

2 eggs, whisked

3 tablespoon coconut oil

½ teaspoon baking powder

4 tablespoon coconut flour

2 tablespoons heavy cream

Method

1.   Mix up vanilla extract and coconut oil.

2.   After this, add whisked eggs, heavy cream, baking powder, and coconut flour.

3.   Stir the mixture with the help of the fork until smooth texture.

4.   Pour the batter into 2 small cake molds.

5.   Pour water in the instant pot and insert the cake molds.

6.   Set "Manual" mode for 5 minutes (High pressure).

7.   Allow the natural pressure release for 5 minutes more.

Nutritional info per serve: calories 363, fat 32.8, fiber 6, carbs 10.4, protein 8.9

Chili Roasted Eggs 25
Chili Verde Soup 49
Chili Zoodles 41
Chinese Beef 66
Cinnamon Prawns 100
Classic Taco Meat 57
Club Salad 83
Coconut Balls 111
Coconut Squid 95
Cod Lime Pieces 96
Cod under the Bagel Spices Crust 98
Cordon Blue Soup 54
Crackle Chicken 85
Cream Cheese Puree 40
Cream Keto Beans 43
Cream of Mushrooms Soup 52
Cream Shrimps 35
Creamy Beef Strips 63
Cremini Mushrooms Stew 41
Crustless Fish Pie 96
Cuban Pork 72
Cumin Chili 64
Cupcake Mugs 26
Cups with Greens 32
Curry Kale Soup 51
Custard Tarts 116

E

Easy and Fast Chicken Drumsticks 93
Easy Taco Stuffing 64
Egg Balls 78
Egg Drop Soup 55
Egg Pate 34
Egg&Cheese 28
Eggplant Lasagna 73
Eggplant Parm 40

F

Fajita Pork Strips 79
Falafel Salad 107
Feta Chicken Drumsticks 87
Feta Stuffed Chicken 26
Filipino Pork 72
Fish Cream Cheese Casserole 101
Fish Nuggets 96
Flax Meal Bread 39
Flounder Baked with Artichokes 99
Flounder Meuniere 97
Flu Soup 53
Fluffy Brulee 114
Frozen Strawberry Cheesecake 118

G

Garden Soup 53
Garlic Asparagus 42
Garlic Butter with Herbs 38
Garlic Italian Sausages 69
Ginger Cabbage 43
Ginger Cod 94
Ginger Meatballs 75
Green Sandwich 92
Ground Beef Okra 58
Ground Salisbury Steak 68

H

Haddock Bake 102
Haddock under Spinach Blanket 94
Ham Muffins 28
Herbed Butter Pork Chops 77
Herbed Chicken Balls 91
Hot BBQ Wings 80

I

Indian Style Chicken 88
Italian Style Kale 44

S

Ropa Vieja 57
Salmon Loaf 98
Salmon Pate 94
Salmon Salad with Feta 47
Salmon with Dill 100
Sausage Puffs 30
Sauteed Green Mix 42
Scallions&Olives Salad 106
Scrambled Eggs Salad 48
Sesame Bok Choy 44
Sesame Zoodle Salad 106
Shirataki Noodle Soup 54
Shredded Pork Stew 79
Shrimp Ragout 102
Sirloin Roast 58
Smoked Paprika Pulled Pork 75
Sour Seabass 101
Southern Okra 105
Spanakopita 29
Spanish Chicken 80
Spanish Style Pork Shoulder 78
Spiced Pudding 110
Spicy Eggs 31
Spicy Fish Balls 101
Steak Soup 50
Steamed Seabass 103
Stuffed Lettuce Boats 35
Succulent Beef Ribs 66
Sugar-Free Coconut Squares 116
Summer Squash Gratin 105
Sweet Ham 71
Sweet Zucchini Crisps 115

T

Tangy Pork 71
Tender Celery Cubes 42
Tender Pork Liver 74
Tender Pork with Salsa Verde 79
Tender Purple Petals 45
Tender Salmon Fillets 103
Thick Beef Gravy 61
Tomatillos Fish Stew 49
Tomato Chicken 86
TSO Chicken Drumsticks 83
Tuna Stuffed Poblanos 100
Turmeric Cauliflower Shred 47
Turmeric Rutabaga Soup 52
Turnip Cake Cups 111
Turnip Roast 109

V

Vanilla Curd 113
Vanilla Liquid Cake 119
Vegan Cream Soup 56
Vegan Pepperoni 104
Vegetable Frittata 28
Vegetable Lasagna with Meat 67
Vinegar Chicken Fillets 81

W

White Mushrooms Poultry Stew 87

Z

Zebra Cakes in Cup 118
Zucchini and Cheese Scones 38
Zucchini Cheese Rings 48
Zucchini Fries 37
Zucchini Hasselback 108
Zucchini Ravioli 39
Zucchini Roll 32